BEDFORD
Villages

Text by the Bedfordshire County Federation of
Women's Institutes
Photographs by Dennis Bidwell

COUNTRYSIDE BOOKS
Newbury, Berkshire

First published 2002
© Photographs – Dennis Bidwell 2002
© Text – Bedfordshire County Federation of Women's Institutes 2002

All rights reserved. No reproduction
permitted without the prior permission
of the publisher:

COUNTRYSIDE BOOKS
3 Catherine Road
Newbury, Berkshire

To view our complete range of books,
please visit us at
www.countrysidebooks.co.uk

ISBN 1 85306 745 8

The front cover photograph shows the Green at Toddington;
the back cover photograph shows St Mary's lychgate,
Northill; and the picture on page 1 was
taken on the Chiltern Hills, near Streatley

Designed by Graham Whiteman

Typeset by Techniset Typesetters, Newton-le-Willows
Produced through MRM Associates Ltd., Reading
Printed in Italy

FOREWORD

I feel sure you will be delighted as I am to see this new all colour book celebrating some of Bedfordshire's most beautiful villages. Along with superb pictures by the celebrated Dennis Bidwell, it brings together many of the accounts of village life contained in *The Bedfordshire Village Book*, first published in 1988.

It provides a timely reminder of how fortunate we are that Bedfordshire can still boast so many unspoilt villages. It tells the story of times past and present and is a lasting record of a county which we can be proud to live in.

Dot Wigg
Chairman
Bedfordshire County Federation of Women's Institutes
Autumn 2002

High Street, Blunham

⌘ AMPTHILL

Ampthill, or Ammetelle as it is recorded in the Domesday book, is situated in the centre of the county, nestling on the side of a wooded Greensand ridge. Despite its past importance, it has retained a village atmosphere.

Lord Fanhope, an uncle to Henry V, made his fortune from the ransoms of French prisoners at Agincourt and eventually acquired Ampthill manor and had a castle built in the parkland.

Ampthill became the favourite hunting seat of King Henry VIII. It is recorded that Anne Boleyn came with the King to the castle in 1532. Queen Catherine of Aragon stayed at the castle for three years whilst a special court was convened at Dunstable Priory Church to look into the legality of her marriage to the King. Catherine refused to attend the court and in 1533 the King secured his divorce. The event is described in Shakespeare's play *King Henry VIII*, Act IV which mentions Ampthill.

In 1542 the King created the Honour of Ampthill, as a way to organise his newly acquired estates in the area.

Oliver Cromwell sold the park to a John Okey, who held it briefly, but after the Restoration King Charles II granted Ampthill to Lord Ashburnham. The castle by

Cottages near Ampthill Park

now was a ruin and a house was built, which later became the property of Lord Ossory. In due course it was acquired by the Duke of Bedford.

In 1947 the Council purchased the parkland. It now provides pitches for sports and a children's playground, but most of all a beautiful place for walking where from the high ground of the ridge there are fine views over the Bedfordshire countryside.

Lovers of architecture will find a walk through Ampthill a very satisfying experience. Four main roads converge at the Market Square, where there can be seen shops with bow-fronted windows and an 18th century arcaded shop.

Nearby is the pump, an obelisk of Portland stone, a gift by Lord Ossory in 1785. This used to have a water trough at its base with a cup on a chain. A market has been held since the 13th century but is now located in a nearby car park.

The White Hart Hotel on the south-west corner of the square has a Georgian frontage but was originally an earlier Tudor building. In the 18th century the local Quarter Sessions were held there. In recent years when some interior work was being carried out a 17th century mural was uncovered on one of the walls. In bygone days the White Hart was the only hotel for miles and coaches would stop there to change horses.

The dominant feature of the square, on the site of the old Moot Hall, is the 19th century brick corner building with a cupola and clock, the whole crowned with a weather vane. Off the square through an archway can be seen the delightful Kings Arms Yard with white-painted timber-framed buildings and on one wall the date 1677 and a fleur de lys inscribed.

Of many fine houses, Avenue House, Church Street is the most notable. It is a Georgian dwelling, built in 1740 and more recently the home of the late Sir Albert Richardson, an architect and a past President of the Royal Academy. A great deal of the restoration work carried out on buildings in the locality was the result of his inspiration.

The local parish church is set back in a small quiet square with the high gabled Feoffee Almshouses to one side and the imposing Georgian Dynevor House on the other.

The church dates from the 14th century. Inside are several brasses and a marble monument to a local inhabitant, Richard Nicolls, who was sent as a commissioner to oversee the lands taken from the Dutch in North America. He received the surrender of Nieu Amsterdam, now New York, and eventually became the first Governor of Long Island. Nicolls returned to England but war broke out again with the Dutch and in a naval battle off the coast of Suffolk at Sole Bay in 1672 he was killed by a cannon-ball which is now incorporated in the monument.

Since the Second World War there has been much residential expansion but the local authorities have designated the surrounding land 'green belt' and much of the centre is conservation area so that the very attractive nature of Ampthill with its park is preserved.

⌘ ASPLEY GUISE

'Holly Hedges and Holy Women'
'Old Maids and Worn Out Parsons'

No one seems to know why these two descriptions of Aspley Guise have been quoted so frequently. Certainly the holly hedges still abound in this large, handsome village situated two miles north of Woburn, in the wooded area through which run the county boundaries of Bedfordshire and Buckinghamshire.

The original village settlement was Saxon (recorded as Aepslea in AD 969), the settlers no doubt being attracted by the dry, sandy soil, abundant woodland and plentiful supply of fresh spring water, an agreeable contrast to the then marshy Bedfordshire Valley. Names on ancient maps – Hogsty End, Water End, Aspley Mill – depict a mainly rural area.

Mentioned in the Domesday Book as having 25 families, the village took the second part of its name from Anselm de Gyse, lord of the manor in 1259. For a short while in the 16th century the manor was the property of Princess Elizabeth (later to become Queen Elizabeth I) but sadly the original manor house fell into disrepair after the Civil War and was demolished in the late 18th century. Even the original church of St Botolph has been altered considerably over the years.

Local landowners were largely responsible for some very fine buildings – Aspley House, designed by Sir Christopher Wren, the White House, now known as the Old House, and later on the Classical Academy (now Guise House), a private boarding school which educated the sons of wealthy families from the surrounding areas.

There was every opportunity for employment both on the land, in service or with the local tradesmen who started various businesses to serve the increasing population. Occupations recorded include blacksmiths, gamekeepers, rat-catchers, millers, dressmakers and cordwainers. Until comparatively recently the village was entirely self-supporting for daily needs. Several butchers, bakers and grocers existed and milk was delivered in churns twice daily. The coming of the railway in 1846 and the building of the local Ridgmont Brickworks, now demolished, later opened up further sources of work.

In later years, at Moore Place in the village square, Captain Courage of the brewing family stabled Shire horses and it is said that the clock above the stables was always kept 5 minutes fast in order that he should be in time to catch his train to London. School children would also know that when the clock struck they had exactly five minutes to run to school.

The 19th century gave Aspley Guise a reputation as 'a healthy resort in which to live due to the dry air and invigorating climate' and many wealthy merchants seeking a country retreat made their homes here, amongst the pine trees.

During the Second World War the village was known as 'the hush-hush village'. The house called the Rookery, together with the transmitting station in nearby

Aspley Guise village centre

Milton Bryan, was taken over by the government as part of the Political Warfare Executive based at Woburn Abbey. Bletchley Park, some five miles away, was used as a de-coding centre for the allied forces and many of the people working there were resident in the village throughout the war.

Perhaps the biggest changes have been the building of the M1 motorway in 1959 and, in more recent years, the development of the new city of Milton Keynes, making communication in all directions so much easier.

⌘ BARTON-LE-CLAY

Barton-Le-Clay (or Barton in the Clay) straddles the A6 about six miles north of Luton. It lies at the end of the Chilterns and the Barton Hills are said to have been Bunyan's inspiration for the Delectable Mountains in *The Pilgrim's Progress*.

The long village street goes back far beyond the time when stagecoaches used to come through on their way from London to Bedford. However, the original village would seem to have been in the area around the parish church of St Nicholas, which dates back to 1180. A number of old houses and cottages still survive in that part of the village, the largest of which are The Bury and The Rectory, both built around the time of Elizabeth I. A fraction of the original village green still exists – bounded by Manor Road, Lime Close and the main Bedford Road.

The oldest building in the village is the parish church of St Nicholas. The original small church was built in the 12th century but the main part of the building is from a century or so later. The tower was added in about 1450. There are some medieval encaustic tiles in the chancel floor, 16th century oak pews with linenfold panels, and the fine roof of the nave with its carved eagles and saints is of interest. The church has eight bells, five from 1604-1743 and three from 1904.

Barton was near the boundary which the invading Danes agreed not to cross when they accepted Danelaw imposed by Alfred the Great after he had defeated them several times in AD 878/9. There was fighting near the village and a rare wild flower – the pasque flower – which is supposed to grow where Danish blood was shed, grows in the region. Another plant, dwarf elder, is also reputed to grow in a similar habitat and is mentioned in the writings of Francis Tavener of Hexton in the early 1600s when he told of a battle fought against the Danes in Dunstall, or Danestall, Fields in Barton. Today this area is Dunstall Road and part of a housing estate.

On the A6, close to Luton, local people are well placed to embrace opportunities other than the motor industry or hat trade that once dominated the village.

⌘ BIDDENHAM

Biddenham is recorded in the Domesday Book as Bideham and although it lies so near to Bedford it has a truly rural atmosphere with thatched cottages, old farm buildings and footpaths leading to the river. The village was primarily a farming community set in the fertile Ouse valley and lies in a loop of the river.

The building of the church was started in the 12th century and illustrates four periods of architecture, Norman, Early English, Decorated and Perpendicular. Two bells have been donated making a peal of eight. The font is 15th century with an octagonal stem and bowl, and there are leper's squints, small apertures to enable the congregation in the side aisles to see the altar.

The path from the corner of Gold Lane near the village green, through fields and passing the village pond, is called the Causeway and was the route for carrying coffins to the church. The pond was put in place for the manor house 600 years ago to provide fresh carp for the table. The dovecote in the next field was built to provide meat. This dated back to William and Mary, and although it was restored and restocked with four pairs of doves in 1932, when there was a grand reopening ceremony, it became dangerous in the late 1970s and was removed.

The main charity of Biddenham was the distribution of bull beef on 21st December, St Thomas's Day. The charity was left by the Boteler family, who owned the village and lived in the manor house in the 16th and 17th centuries. Effigies of William and Ursula Boteler are in the church. The manor house in those days was at Old Ford End, down by the river, a fine stone building with a stone walled garden.

It was the practice to buy a beast at the Christmas Fat Stock Show and keep it at one of the farms for a week before it was slaughtered. On the great day, the farm workers stopped work at 12 o'clock and made for the farm where the beast had been killed. Here the farmer's wife and helpers had taken the liver, kidneys and steaks and prepared a great fry-up. This was eaten with plenty of potatoes and new bread and washed down with as much home-brewed beer as they could drink. While this was going on, the women were picking up their joints of beef – adults and children over 16 years old received four pounds and the children two pounds each. The last distribution of beef took place during the Second World War.

Until 1915 the village hall was a straw barn, but during the First World War, when the Black Watch troops were billeted locally, the barn was converted into a canteen for them. After the war the barn was given by the Biddenham estate to the village.

The craft of lace making is still popular. In earlier times young girls attended the village school in the mornings and a lace making school in the afternoons. Thatching has been a local craft for many years. The local blacksmith carrying on his craft used to be a sight to see.

In the 19th century, a local wit made up a fictitious custom, which he placed in Biddenham, and published in a county paper, and at the time fooled quite a few people. In it he said that in olden times the people of Biddenham observed a quaint old custom each year on 22nd September. A procession went round the

Thatched cottages in Biddenham

village, the leader carrying a white rabbit decorated with a scarlet ribbon in honour of St Agatha. All the young unmarried women who chanced to meet the procession extended the first two fingers of the left hand and pointing to the rabbit recited 'Gustin Gustin (St Augustine) lacks a bier, maidens maidens bury him here.' They were then supposed to receive a mental picture of their future husband. This was a ceremony said to date from the time of the first Crusade.

⌘ BILLINGTON

To many people Billington is just a long haul up and swift descent down, as the village is situated on a steep hill. To those who live here, it is straggly, but pretty. It is typical of hundreds of small villages in England, a small pocket of life down the centuries.

The hilltop of Billington was almost certainly a fortified earthwork of ancient peoples, a good signalling post and a lookout for the old Icknield Way. Billendon, as it was known then, was first mentioned in written history in 1196 and was then a hamlet, part of the manor of Leighton. A family by the name of de Billenden lived here and owned property from the Middle Ages until the 16th century.

The little church, dedicated to St Michael and All Angels, stands at the top of the hill, on a very old foundation, and is the central point of the village, looking out onto a lovely view with Linslade and Leighton Buzzard in the distance. The chapel of Billendon is first mentioned in 1277 and although the piscina and the west

Billington

window arch date from the 13th century, much of the rest is greatly restored and there is little trace of the original building.

At one time there were also two chapels in the village, but one has been demolished and the other is now a home. Like many others this village has lost its main amenities, the village shop, post office and school, although the buildings remain as houses. One can recognise the school, which has kept its character, but the shop has blended in with other cottages in the village.

⌘ BLETSOE

Bletsoe is a small village seven miles north of Bedford, just off the A6 trunk road. It stands on rising ground east of a bend in the river Ouse and well out of the way of floods.

The present church is at the top of the village, built on the site of an earlier building in the 13th century and restored in the 19th century. It is an irregular cruciform shape with a central tower with a clock containing a peal of bells. Visitors take some time to work out why it is so much smaller inside than out! There is a chapel devoted to the St John family and an alabaster tomb dating from the end of the 16th century showing Lord and Lady St John and their nine children.

Just across the lane, Bletsoe Castle is not the turreted building many expect to see. Originally a motte and bailey castle, the only indication of the previous imposing building and grounds is the remains of the moat and the steep mounds thrown up for defence. Of the many notable occupants of the castle, the best known is Margaret Beaufort, mother of Henry VII. In the present garden is a 16th century bridge, probably built over what was left of the moat at the entrance to a

Bletsoe seen from The Avenue

large Elizabethan manor house. Today, though large, the house is much smaller than the original building, having had the top storey removed. It stands proudly at the top of the village overlooking farmland not much changed over the centuries.

There are views from the castle toward North End, where Gilbert's Cottage, Northend Farm and the farm cottages were built all at about the same time as the castle. There are other, even older dwellings in the village, those in Old Way, Top Row, and Pixie Cottage in particular.

A secret passage is said to run from the castle and church to The Cottage and thence to the Falcon Inn and the river, but most present day village dwellers go down to that hostelry by the footpath! In the 1830s the poet Edward Fitzgerald used to stay at the Falcon and said it was 'the cleanest, the sweetest, the civilest, the quietest, the liveliest . . .' and it still lives up to that reputation.

Further information as to earlier residents of Bletsoe came to light when the new rectory, now The Grange, was being built in the 1930s. Among the finds were 2nd and 3rd century coins and a beautiful silver spoon with a delicately curved handle, as well as a quantity of skeletons.

The Second World War brought unexpected visitors to stay in this quiet village. American servicemen arrived and nightly the sound of bombers setting off for Europe from surrounding airfields was heard. These transatlantic visitors do return with their families to see the village they once knew and find it not so much altered.

Postwar house building changed Bletsoe. Expansion of the airfield swallowed Whitwick End, while new houses were built at Bourne End. In the village some old cottages and one of the terraced rows disappeared to be replaced by new properties lining one side of The Avenue and by a splendid village hall.

Present day Bletsoe is neat and tidy. Although the school has long since closed there is a growing number of young people. Village societies abound and celebrations take place in the village field, with its views across the valley of the Ouse towards the spire of Sharnbrook church and the distant blur of Odell Woods.

⌘ BLUNHAM

More than 20 different ways of spelling Blunham have been found. The second part of the name is probably from Old English *hamm* 'land in a river bend'. The first has long been recognised as a personal name, presumably the name of the man who founded the settlement and the most recent opinion is that it was Bluwa who chose as his 'hamm' the banks of the Ivel, not far from its confluence with the Ouse at Tempsford, where the marauding Danes were defeated in AD 920. This part of the country continued to suffer from Danish attacks. In 1009 Danish horsemen advanced into Oxfordshire and made their way back to their ships at Tempsford, destroying by fire as they went. So Blunham must have suffered in those days.

However, there must have been some years of peace before Blunham is mentioned in writing for the first time, in the Domesday Book. After the Norman Conquest of England in 1066, King William I divided the lands of Blunham into three parts. One went to St Edmund's Abbey, in what is now called Bury St Edmunds, so it is understandable that when the church was built in the following century it should have been dedicated to St Edmund. Great families left no mark until the manor came into the hands of the Grey family in 1389.

It is not surprising that the Greys and their heirs should have left their mark on the village since they continued as landlords until the beginning of the 20th century and bequeathed the advowson to Balliol College, Oxford, only in 1921. Their memorials are in the church together with those of other important families such as the Bromsalls and the Thorntons of Moggerhanger. However, the Greys' main seat was at Wrest Park, Silsoe, only 10 miles from Blunham, and so there was no permanent family residence in Blunham.

There were gentry living at Blunham House, built in about 1720, a sober undistinguished building set in a small, rather decayed park. They were magistrates and kept the peace but, particularly as the rectors were generally non-resident in the 18th century, Blunham seems to have lacked the close control of the lord of the manor. The parish's most famous incumbent, John Donne, 1621-31, was also Dean of St Paul's Cathedral in London, so he was non-resident, but he certainly paid summer visits to his living and felt so affectionate towards it that he gave it a fine silver chalice.

Blunham continued to grow in the area around the church by the river bank. It was a township with the usual complement of craftsmen and husbandmen, petty officials such as the constable, the ale-conners, the jurymen and the bailiffsmen, who all pursued their complaints and grievances in the manorial court. By the end of the 15th century the more respectable ones at any rate had a social centre for their lives in the Brotherhood of the Holy Trinity, which had its chapel in the parish church and its own house in which the brothers and sisters held feasts.

The Reformation brought changes. The Brotherhood was dissolved, its house became the courthouse and the beautiful alabaster statues in the church were smashed, perhaps at the instigation of George Joye, a typical Bedfordshire iconoclast, who became rector in 1549. There seems to have been a Protestant spirit in Blunham in the 1540s which manifested itself a hundred years later in the Commonwealth when a Puritan minister intruded into the living. The Baptists were certainly active at this time; five Blunham men were imprisoned with John Bunyan in Bedford. Their present meeting house was built in 1751.

The parish was enclosed in 1799 and so the appearance of Blunham was beginning to change, but it was the 19th century that, here as elsewhere, brought the changes which have largely shaped present day Blunham. The building of the railway cut off the view of the village from the south, leaving only the top of the church tower visible over the embankment, and necessitated the building of

Station Road to replace the path across the fields below Blunham House. The church was 'restored' and enlarged in 1862 and about the same time a school was built. The prosperity of market gardening led to the construction of large houses on The Hill, Barford Road and at Grange Road, in the white brick so popular in the 1880s. The Square was now lined with public houses and Mr Judd's stores.

The First World War accelerated the end of that Victorian era. The gentry left Blunham House, council houses were built along Station and Barford Roads. The population declined. Even the railway expired in 1968, but by that time new houses were being built on what had been agricultural land. The school, burnt down in 1971, was rebuilt, alternative centres of employment were created and the population rose once again. The bus service to Bedford and Sandy increased. Commuting, begun earlier in the century, became the norm.

⌘ BROMHAM

The limestone village of Bromham lies three miles west of Bedford by the river Ouse and is approached via a stone bridge with 26 arches, which is scheduled as an Ancient Monument.

The mill, recorded in the Domesday Book, is now owned by the County Council, with machinery in working order and open to the public with a picnic area nearby.

Prior to 1924 when Bromham Hall was sold, the whole village was owned by the family at the Hall. An interesting variety of trees grow in the parkland.

The 13th century parish church, built of limestone, is approached through the park. Interesting monuments include a 15th century brass to the Wydville family and a marble statue of a recumbent knight, Sir Lewis Dyve, whose grandson, another Sir Lewis, an ardent Royalist, swam the river to avoid capture by the Roundheads in 1642.

The happy ghosts of children are sometimes heard playing in the churchyard. Some experts think that cropmarks around the church indicate that houses were built there and that the village later moved.

Miss Elianore Rice Trevor, who owned the hall in the latter part of the 19th century, was a formidable lady who cared for the 300 souls in the village under her domain. She sent 'the bundle' containing baby clothes to all new mothers, and in 1861 opened a school. Her girls were provided with a uniform, in winter of blue serge dresses, red capes and a hat, while in summer, print dresses, a holland cape and a hat were worn. Miss Rice Trevor bequeathed £12 each year for 12 girls attending Sunday School and church. This money was to buy their uniform when they went into domestic service. Tradition has it that the water of Grove Spring in Bromham Park has healing powers for sore eyes and sprains.

In 1896, entrepreneur, W. H. Allen arrived in the village and built Bromham House after founding his engineering company in Bedford. At one period, during

Bromham Bridge and Mill

the 20th century, the House formed part of the Bromham Hospital for the mentally handicapped which provided employment for local people over many years. After its closure the House became a private residence again.

⌘ CADDINGTON

Caddington is a large village situated near to the Hertfordshire border. Its earliest written record is a will dated *c*.1050.

Zouches Farm dates back to the 16th century, before which it is believed the lord of the manor had his dwelling there. Folklore has it that Dick Turpin, being chased by the law and knowing his horse would give him away, backed it down one of the wells to avoid capture. The land is still a farm and nowadays, bringing it right in the 21st century, supports a communications mast which can be seen for miles around.

As with most historic villages, Caddington is justifiably proud of its church. The two canons sent by St Paul's Cathedral to manage the two manors or estates have on their chair seats in the cathedral the names 'Caddington Major' and 'Minor'. If you look these out you will find one of the workmen had difficulty with his spelling.

It was decided in 1913 to purchase more burial land as people were having to be buried at Aley Green. Looking back to the history books, references were made to a parsonage built in 1539 and bequeathed in 1546 by George Rotherham to the church and parish. During the 16th/17th century it became the poor man's house (poorhouse) and by 1742 it had become one of two workhouses in the village. This building would have stood where the extended cemetery plot is now situated.

A schoolhouse was built 1859 and a National School. There were always the regular absentee scholars at harvest time. The Howe brothers would bring their threshers through the village to a parade of schoolchildren. Everyone with a dog would be available for corn cutting to catch the rats as they ran for cover.

Whipsnade Zoo in 1927 required electricity, which would be routed from Luton through Caddington. When electricity came to Caddington, Vicar Greaves called upon the services of his friend Sir Albert Richardson from Ampthill, for his ideas as to how the church should be lit and the ensuing system of overhead floodlighting was reckoned to be very advanced for its time.

Vicar Greaves used the vicarage court to teach village children how to play tennis; he also used the hall for hockey instruction. After a number of windows were broken he set about raising money for a village hall. The hall was named in memory of John Collings Wells of Caddington Hall, who was awarded the VC during the battle of Gallipoli in the First World War.

Caddington had a Roman refuse tip opposite Little Green Lane and at Castle End remains were found of flint tools showing that this was a place where they were made. More recent are the clay pits. The clay is supposed to be of the finest in the country. The farmers owned the pits, the deepest being 15 feet. This clay was made into bricks, Caddington Greys. The trouble was the weather – if it was not fine men did not earn a wage at all. There were 17 pits in all. Cottage industry for the wives consisted of hat work for Luton.

The bakery was opposite the green. It is still there under the road. The shop was at street level and the ovens underground. When the shop was levelled the ovens were left as they were. Villagers here, as in most other villages, used the ovens at Christmas for a small fee to cook their Christmas meat.

Caddington has grown enormously in recent years. The M1 is very handy for commuting to London. How different in 1050, when it was all thick forest!

⌘ CAMPTON

Campton is a small village lying just to the south of the main A507 Shefford to Ampthill road.

There are some interesting old buildings here, notably the manor house, which was built in about 1591 and is timber-framed with gabled wings. The Ventris family were here for about 200 years from the 1550s, and during the Civil War Sir Charles Ventris was shot at in his own home by a Cromwellian soldier, leaving a bullet hole in the wall. The 12th century Chicksands Priory, formerly used by the US Air Force, is now a British Defence and Security Centre, but the public has a chance to look around from time to time.

Campton Manor House

The 13th century parish church of All Saints has been the source of an upsurge of community activity. It is an attractive church with some interesting memorials to the Osborns of Chicksands Priory.

⌘ CARDINGTON

Cardington is a small, picturesque village three miles to the south-east of Bedford. To the casual observer, it appears to be a sleepy little place that sets its own pace. The casual observer, in this case, would not be wrong!

Residents of Cardington have seen many changes over the last few years, all of which have happened gradually but each of which has taken away a small piece of Cardington's soul – the slow drop in the number of pupils at the village school and its eventual closure, for example. The school had been open since the 19th century, when the children had to sit back to back to keep warm and the ink used to freeze in the inkwells!

The village focuses upon a large green and residents can remember when majestic elm trees used to dominate the landscape. Sadly, Dutch elm disease took its toll back in the 1970s and any trees now found on the green are relatively young. The grand holm oak tree to the north of the green still stands proud, however.

Cardington is a village steeped in history and character. Many of its houses date back to the 17th century and ghost stories are quite commonplace among the

Near the village green in Cardington

residents. The crash of the R101 airship which took off from Cardington airfield in the 1930s added its fair share of stories to the collection, and several houses are said to be haunted by members of the crew who have come back to search for their loved ones.

As well as being famous for its aircraft hangars and the fated R101 airship, Cardington has connections too with the prison reformer John Howard, who lived during the 18th century and after whom the village hall, or the Howard Reading Room, is named. Being an estate village – linked to the Whitbread family – means that living in sleepy Cardington is like stepping back in history; it is as though life here has been caught in a time warp.

⌘ CLAPHAM

Clapham is still a village, in spite of being only one and a half miles north of Bedford on the busy A6. It is long and straggly, the main road running almost parallel to the meandering river Ouse.

Part of Clapham Park is now owned by Bedfordshire County Council as demonstration woodlands. In 1873, John Usher built Clapham Park House for James Howard, the founder of Britannia Iron Works in Bedford, which made agricultural machinery. The only other large house is Woodlands in Green Lane.

In 1973 an archaeological dig uncovered remains of three manor houses, an Elizabethan one on top of early Tudor walls, while below these were medieval tiles. A cellar contained skeletons of five hunting dogs and a wild boar and there were also remains of a circular dovecote. Later excavations on the other side of the school revealed evidence of a Roman field system, with remnants of Roman and Iron Age pottery.

The village has grown tremendously since the 1930s, particularly since the Royal Aircraft Establishment came in 1950. At one time there was a farm in the centre of the village where the shops now stand and a small recreation field behind the shops. On the site of the playing fields and the community centre there was a wheatfield, and at the south end of the shops the village pond and the well. At the bottom of Green Lane there was a field with a pond in the corner. There were no houses to the south of the school, apart from the cottage on the opposite corner and the old thatched cottage which was the lodge for Woodlands and housed the coachman or chauffeur.

The river was visible all the way through the village. In Oakley Road, a path to the river allowed cattle to have a drink before the drovers completed the long trek into Bedford Market. Private houses have been built all along the west side of the A6 and the general public can only reach the river through Riverside Gardens or at the ford.

An important feature of village life was Clapham Feast Day, held in the summer, when friends and relatives walked from Bedford and surrounding villages to a field near the club in the centre, where there was a fair and races for the children. Not so popular were the annual floods, usually about February, when the river overflowed and met the surface water coming down from the hills. People living near the river would have to live upstairs, sometimes for two weeks. The river was dredged and deepened in the 1930s, much to the relief of residents.

⌘ CLIFTON

Clifton was once a village of considerable Anglo Saxon importance and archaeological remains were discovered indicating that an early settlement was thriving about 1086, thus confirming the entry in the Domesday Book.

Life in Clifton has changed considerably in recent years, but the architecture of days past can still be seen in such buildings as Holly Cottage, which dates from the 17th century. This used to be a Quaker meeting house. Quakers were persecuted at this time and in 1670 a Clifton Quaker had his goods seized to the value of £2 for attending an illegal meeting. Clifton Cottage, which originally was two cottages, has deeds going back to 1638. The church of All Saints, which is of particular medieval interest, dates from 1300.

Farming was the principal work in the village and this must have produced many thirsty throats as there were six public houses at one time! Other trades to be found were a thriving mineral water factory, which lasted until 1947, only having to close for a short time during the Second World War due to a shortage of sugar. Bottles with marble stoppers are still being dug up in local gardens. Wooden farm implements were made in the village by the Slater family and samples of their work can still be seen in the Wardown Museum at Luton. Straw plaiting was also an important feature of life, children starting this work as early as eight years old.

The village pond is another well-loved feature of the village and to one side is a cottage which was originally two almshouses, with one door having the words 'The Little Gleaner' and the other 'The Sower' above it. Clifton also had its workhouse and in 1822 the inmates were served such dainty dishes as water gruel, broth and pudding and beef to sustain them.

Today many new estates have grown up in Clifton but it still retains its village attraction.

⌘ CLOPHILL

Clophill is a popular, pretty village surrounded by woodlands and delightful walks. Chestnuts are gathered in plenty during October and November.

In the late 1800s and early 1900s Clophill had twelve shops, three blacksmiths and six public houses. It was renowned for its straw plaiting and a factory was in the High Street. The ladies each day would take their plait to the Flying Horse public house, from where a carrier would take it to Luton to be made into hats. There was also a plait school in the old reading room.

The Clophill Charity still survives in the village – left to the Clophill labourers by one Thomas Dearman. The story goes that he was employed in one of the bigger

Clophill village green

houses in this area. One day his mother arrived at the door of where he worked as a valet or manservant. She was begging for help but Thomas turned her away. But on his death he left all he had to Clophill's poor and needy. He was buried in the old churchyard on the hill.

It is said that anyone who misbehaved in Silsoe was banished to Clophill to live in the Slade. There is a pound and a lock-up on the village green for animals and drunks. Also at the top of the Slade, animals were taken for slaughter. This is the meaning of Knives Lane, so called today.

On St Thomas's Day each year, the widows of the village would go around to the bigger houses begging. They were invited in and given food and clothing, this day being known as Goodening Day.

Clophill has two churches, one in the village dating from 1845 and the old one on the hill out of the village. Services used to be held twice a year in the old church, until thieves stripped the roof of its lead. Now green grass surrounds the ruins of this lovely little church.

⌘ COLMWORTH

Colmworth is about seven miles north-east of Bedford. It is a straggling village spread over a distance of seven miles with many Ends – Church End, Chapel End, Channel End – and Roothams Green, Begwary and The City, a curious name which perhaps began as a joke as there were so few houses.

A mill was working in the village in 1227 but was moved elsewhere. There was also a post-type mill working until 1906.

Colmworth has always been a peaceful and agricultural village with the people working their own small pieces of land with a few pigs, poultry and maybe a cow. It was not until crawler tractors and strong machinery became available, helping to drain and cultivate the heavy land, that the village moved to larger scale farming.

The old manor house was pulled down in 1609. It was rebuilt as a huge, rambling place and in 1671 they were paying tax on its 20 hearths. Again, it was half pulled down and today it still has timbers from the older house and the remains of a medieval moat.

Down a cul-de-sac stands the church of St Denys with its tall spire. The church stands on a rise of 230 feet above sea level, overlooking the Ouse valley. The present church was begun in 1426 and building was completed in 1430, quite an achievement for that century. A unique feature of the building work was the fact that the chancel and nave were built together; they are of rare scale and beauty and have many interesting features. One such is the north chancel window, the only piece of medieval glass to survive. It depicts 'The Angel' to commemorate St Catherine. Other remaining fragments are from the high parts of the windows and these are all that survived the Civil War in Cromwell's time.

At one time there were no less than five public houses in the village. The Three

Colmworth

Horseshoes was opposite the blacksmith's. The Old White Swan had shove-ha'penny, darts and a piano. Both these old pubs are now private residences. A very early off-licence was at Begwary, where you could take your own jug for beer. Only the Wheatsheaf which dates from at least the 15th century or earlier now remains.

In 1930 eight council houses were built on the old cricket field. Now bungalows and houses have been added all along the main road and down many of the Ends. But, for those who wish, you can still walk through open fields (keeping to paths), and Green Lane, being part of an old carriage road, sees dog lovers and horses only.

⌘ COTTON END

On the crest of the hill in the depths of Exeter Wood, lies a mound measuring 90 feet across with a surrounding ditch. This has been identified as a likely site for a Norman watchtower, well positioned for observing the Ouse valley. Although no remains can be seen above ground, coins dating from AD 200 onwards have been found in the fields suggesting links with the Romans. The name 'Exeter Wood' is a reminder that much of the land was owned by Lord Exeter until the late 1800s.

The Manor Farm House, built in the 16th century, was originally an 'E' shaped Elizabethan house. Unfortunately at some time it suffered from the ravages of a fire which destroyed the south wing. The house still retains some Tudor windows and massive chimney stacks, an interesting square porch, and a dovecote at the back.

Three old cottages still stand in Bell Lane and these have strong links with John Bunyan; it is believed he may actually have preached from there.

In the early 1900s, Cotton End boasted two pork butchers, a famous sausage maker, two shoemakers, a baker and two hurdle makers. There was also a lace pillow maker, a lace bobbin maker and a policeman. The shoemaker made hand sewn boots, stout and thick, sewn with waxed twine, for work on the land. The bread was delivered to surrounding villages and on Christmas Day the bakehouse fires were stoked up to cook dinners, as the villagers would take their joints and poultry along to be cooked in the oven.

⌘ CRANFIELD

The first record of Cranfield (then Cranfeldga) was in AD 918 when Ailwin Niger granted a manor at Cranfield to the monks of Ramsey Abbey in Huntingdonshire. The manor was held by the abbey until 1539, when, on the dissolution of the monasteries, it reverted to the Crown. The name means clearing of the forest occupied by cranes.

The old pump stands on the village green in Cranfield

The first stone church was built in the middle of the 12th century. Prior to this there was a wood and thatch building built by the monks of Ramsey Abbey. The present clock on the church tower was installed in 1897 to commemorate Queen Victoria's Jubilee.

William Wheeler, formerly rector of Cranfield, left the parish church because of a conflict of principles. He became a dissenter and then the first minister of the Baptist church in 1660. Later on he was in prison with John Bunyan.

In the early 19th century a Cranfield woman known as Nanny Draper was said to have the 'evil eye' and was given presents in order to prevent her 'witching' the farm stock. It is believed that Cranfield had a ghost called Lady Snagg, who rode on a headless horse.

There is a place called Holy Well, where there is still a well with a hawthorn tree hanging over it: the well water was said to cure sore eyes

⌘ DUNTON

Dunton is situated about three miles from Biggleswade and very close to both the Cambridgeshire and Hertfordshire county boundaries. The village is dominated by its church, St Mary Magdalene, which has been in existence for the last 750 years. The tower stands tall over the surrounding countryside. During the church's long history there have been several periods of restoration, the tower itself having been rebuilt in 1861. A new roof for the chancel was partly paid for by an ancestor of Princess Diana, one of the Earl Spencers. The roof is supported by 12 angels each playing a musical instrument – these are rumoured to have come from a Biggleswade church in 'mysterious circumstances'.

As with many other villages, Dunton is no longer self-sufficient. In 1871 it had two blacksmiths, three thatchers, a needlemaker, and a cobbler as well as boasting five public houses, where villagers gathered for a pint or two of good ale. And, of course, they had their own bakehouse which survived until quite recent years to supply them with bread. Pure heaven was the aroma of fresh baked bread and buns; none of that steam-baked bread for Dunton! The good old brick oven also came in handy at Christmas, when a few lucky villagers had their Christmas 'bird' cooked for them. Unfortunately today the bakehouse is no longer in use and the oven is crumbling away now that the fire has gone out forever.

Of course, Dunton is famous for its 'docks' – a pond on the outskirts of the village, so called because the steam engines would stop there to fill up with water. The steam engine and cable plough are part of Dunton's farming history.

Older villagers remember the local gamekeeper who would gallop his horse through the streets pistol or shotgun in hand and who once turned up, horse and all, to join a dance being held in the village hall!

Dunton includes the hamlets of Millow and Newton. Millow was at one time believed to be a bigger settlement than Dunton itself. Newton Grove remains, but

The church of St Mary Magdalene, Dunton

the 17th century cottages and farm buildings at Newton Bury are derelict. The moat which surrounded the Bury cottages is still clearly visible.

⌘ EATON BRAY

Soon after the Norman baron William de Cantilupe had acquired the manor of Eaton, he built himself a castle. This was in 1221, and at about the same time the beautiful north and south arcades of the church were erected. Only the water-filled moat remains to mark the site of the castle.

The church, however, still contains some of the original carving in Totternhoe stone together with fine wrought ironwork on the south door. It was partly rebuilt in the 15th century by Reginald Bray, who was appointed lord of the manor by Henry VII. He was the chief architect of St George's Chapel, Windsor, and many examples of his skilful design are to be seen in the church. It was from him that the village derived its name, Eaton Bray.

Many fine old timber-framed houses and cottages can still be seen in the village, although most of the thatched roofs have been replaced by tiles. The village pond on the Market Square was filled in many years ago and the blacksmith's house and forge which adjoined it has now become a desirable residence, called The Old Forge. The mill stream running under the old flour mill forms both county and village boundaries between Eaton Bray and the neighbouring village of Edlesborough, which is in Buckinghamshire.

26

Eaton Bray's ancient water-filled moat

Eaton Bray's history was centred on farming and straw plaiting as well as stone carving and flour milling. Extensive plum orchards produced prunes, the skins of which were used by Luton's hat industry for dyeing felt. When the fruit was ripe pickers converged on the orchards to gather it as quickly as possible and many tons were collected each year. During the Second World War prunes were much in demand for cooking and jam making.

Towards the end of the 19th century W. E. Wallace started a nursery which provided much needed employment for the villagers. This was greatly expanded in the 1920s and specialised in growing carnations, which were sent to London by rail from nearby Stanbridgeford. Now the acres of old glasshouses have been demolished to make way for the dwelling houses and most of the plum orchards have grown a crop of small estates.

At the turn of the century Eaton Bray was reputed to have a public house every 200 yards. One which has disappeared, called The Labour in Vain, had a hand-painted sign depicting a woman trying to scrub a small black child white.

In the past villagers had the choice of a wide range of shops including two bakers, several grocers, a general store and sweetshop, draper, newsagent, fish shop, post office and a barber's shop, all situated in the High Street. Daily shopping became a pleasant way of meeting friends and making new acquaintances.

⌘ EGGINGTON

Eggington (possibly 'Ecca's hill') has always been a small, self-contained village, and settlement can be traced back to prehistoric times. From Roman and medieval buildings on Haydon Hill, to thatched cottages with wattle and daub walls and oak beams, dwellings have improved through the centuries. Later cottages were built with local red bricks, until the brickworks opened in 1844 and clay was worked in the village, fired in the kilns and the yellow gault bricks used to build the larger houses, school, two chapels and the vicarage.

Situated in the south-west corner of Bedfordshire, Eggington is not far from the market town of Leighton Buzzard. It is lucky to be set away from the main A4012 and to have escaped the urban development of nearby towns, so retaining much of its charm and character.

Village crafts have changed over the years from straw plaiting to knitting, spinning and weaving wool, lace making and crochet.

Industries years ago were mainly concerned with farms and country life, as the many horses needed blacksmith's shops and grooms; gamekeepers, gardeners and servants worked at the big houses; while thatchers, hedgers, ditchers, ploughboys and shepherds worked in the fields. The village brewery and alehouses provided refreshment for those men who had worked up a thirst in the open air all day. There was also a carpenter and joiner's workshop in the centre of the village, which made cabinets, coffins, gates, fences, and all the woodwork for the rebuilding of St Michael and All Angels church, after a fire in 1876. Down Nursery Lane a sandpit was opened in 1931 and the good quality sand was taken by horse and cart to the roadside, loaded onto lorries and then taken to be sold in London. When the men were called up for war service in 1939, the pit had to close. There were several bakehouses, shops and a post office in the village, but with easier

Eggington's village centre

transport by bus and car to nearby towns, these have gradually closed.

Built in 1881, the village school was open for just over 100 years, and welcomed many children evacuated from London during the Second World War. However, the school was a Grade II listed building and so needed to be preserved as part of the village scene. Soon the old school began a new life as a much needed village hall and community centre.

⌘ ELSTOW

Judith, the niece of William the Conqueror, founded the Benedictine abbey or convent in Elstow (or Helenestowe as it was known in Norman times) about 1078, as atonement for causing the death of her husband. The convent flourished, although not without some problems. In 1530 the Bishop of Lincoln had to reprimand the abbess for allowing the sisters to wear low-cut red dresses, and 'entertaining'!

The abbey was surrendered to Henry VIII, and in 1553 the nave was shortened by two bays, and the central tower, transcepts, chancel and lady chapel were removed (the present abbey church is less than half the length of the original abbey). Sir Humphrey Radcliffe had received the abbey in 1553, and in 1616 Sir Edward Radcliffe sold the abbey and estate to Sir Thomas Hillersdon, who had Hillersdon House built on the site of cloisters and convent buildings. It is the Hillersdon ruins that are often misdescribed as the abbey ruins.

In 1628 John Bunyan was born in the parish of Elstow and he was baptised in the abbey church on 30th November of that year. His mother, Margaret, and sister, also Margaret (1644), his father, Thomas (1676), and step-mother, Ann (1680), are all buried in Elstow churchyard. (Records of 1885 state that their 'graves cannot be identified'.) He was born near Harrowden, at Pesselynton Furlong, and a stone erected in 1951 marks the site of his birthplace. A wooden plaque marks the site of 'Bunyan's Cottage'.

Also buried in the churchyard, in an unmarked, but known

The Moot Hall at Elstow

position, is Ann Harding, the lace maker featured on many early postcards. When Rev. Stanley Victor Hartley was buried, he was laid facing west, so that on the 'Day of Judgement when every body rises' he would be facing his congregation.

Moot Hall (or Green House), situated on the village green, was originally a market house used during the 'fairs'. It was later used as the meeting place for Elstow manor court, and then for nonconformist worship. The building dates from about 1500.

On the east side of the High Street stands 'Bunyan's Mead', a row of half-timbered, jettied buildings dating from the 16th to 17th centuries. All of the buildings were sold by Whitbread estates for just £1 in the early 1970s, and have been completely renovated in their original form, ie all the pebble-dash rendering removed to expose half-timbered stucco construction.

⌘ EYEWORTH

Although there has been a settlement here for at least 600 years very little remains of the older houses except for Church Farm, which dates back to the 17th century. The majority of the houses in this tiny village now date from the late 19th century. The church, however, was built in the 14th and 15th centuries. In 1967 during a storm the church was struck by lightning, demolishing its steeple, and since the insurance was insufficient to restore it to its former state it was replaced by a much smaller version and the balance of the money used to put heating into the church.

Noteworthy inhabitants of the past include Sir Edmund Anderson, who was a judge at the trial of Mary Queen of Scots, and the widow of Francis Bacon, who died at Eyeworth in 1650, having outlived her husband by 30 years.

There were various skirmishes in this area between the forces of Oliver Cromwell and the Royalists. Oliver Cromwell is reputed to have visited Eyeworth himself and to have been responsible for damaging some of the effigies in the church.

There was a long-believed story that there was a bushel of gold buried in a grassed field behind one of the farms. However, this has been ploughed during recent years and nothing found. With the advent of metal detectors treasure hunters arrived but the only things unearthed were metal buttons from the uniforms of soldiers billeted there during the Second World War!

⌘ FELMERSHAM

The history of Felmersham village goes back beyond Saxon times, when it is believed there was a settlement on the raised ground south of the river Ouse. The village was mentioned in the Domesday Book, originally named as Falmeresham or Flammeresham. The church and the tithe barn are the oldest buildings in the village. The church, once connected with Trinity College, Cambridge, is regarded as one of the finest examples of the Early English style to be found in the county of Bedfordshire; the tithe barn, once reputed to be owned by monks from Lenton Priory, has now been converted into four dwellings.

Life in Felmersham was more that of a farming community than it is today. At harvest time the Harvest Home was cause for great celebration in the village. The first farmer home would go round the village with his cart, gathering a crowd of men, women and children; boughs would be cut to decorate the carts which then paraded round the village with the occupants singing 'Holler Boy Holler, Harvest Home', calling for refreshments on their way. The Harvest Supper held in the club room in the Sun Inn was given by the squire and this took place with singing, dancing and the drinking of ale. People would come from neighbouring villages for the Harvest Thanksgiving, many having to walk.

Early in the 20th century the squire held his annual Ram Sale, which was a major event, being a social gathering as well as a sale. People came from near and far and consumed large quantities of beer and bread and cheese (no doubt remembering to buy the odd ram or two!). The occasion was rounded off with a smoking concert.

Felmersham Feast was traditionally held on the first Sunday after the 26th August. It centred on the Sun Inn, with roundabouts in Harvest Yard (the site of the present houses numbered 1–6 in Grange Road). By the 1930s the traditional Feasts had been replaced by garden fetes, which were introduced by the owner of the Grange, Sir Richard Wells. Over the years Felmersham has become more of a dormitory village than an agricultural community, but nevertheless has retained its close community spirit.

Felmersham village

⌘ FLITTON

The village of Flitton with the hamlet of Greenfield is situated about nine miles to the south of Bedford and is mentioned in the Domesday Book as being in the Flitt Hundred.

The parish church is built of local brown sandstone and stands on a small rise in the centre of the village. It was built in the 15th century under the patronage of Edmund, Lord Grey of Wrest Park, Silsoe and is dedicated to St John the Baptist. The building is somewhat unusual in that the east window cannot be seen from the outside as it is enclosed by the De Grey Mausoleum, again giving a link with Wrest Park and the family, the first burial there being that of Henry Grey in 1545. It contains some very ornate tombs, with excellent carved effigies, making it well worth visiting.

The river Flitt which flows through both Flitton and Greenfield is about 16 miles in length. It rises in the grounds of Woburn Abbey and continues in an easterly direction to south of Biggleswade, where it joins the river Ivel. The main uses of the Flitt were to operate the mill wheels and to irrigate and drain the surrounding market gardening land. The mill at Greenfield was working until 1956 and was demolished to make way for housing in 1970.

In the 19th century Flitton and Greenfield were significant strawberry growing centres. The fields on both sides of the main road were filled with strawberry plants and in the season wagons could be seen collecting strawberries to take to Luton, Bedford and London. In the 1920s a blight destroyed all the plants and, unfortunately, they were never replaced. Market gardening is still carried on today, but with modern methods of agriculture fewer people are needed on the land.

⌘ FLITWICK

'Small is beautiful' applied to Flitwick many years ago, noted in the Domesday Book as a 'hamlet on the river Flitt' with 16 inhabitants. Huge development has overtaken it now, but the old village memories remain.

In the main the railway, which Flitwick was fortunate to keep during the Beeching era, has contributed to the growth, a great attraction for commuters. It was allowed to continue due to the immense amount of local produce which was transported daily to Covent Garden.

Off the main throughfare stands the 13th century church of St Peter & St Paul, in remarkably good condition and complete with a lepers' window where they took communion without contact with the congregation. Old hassocks have been replaced with gaily woven stitched ones donated by many organisations and in memory of loved ones. Behind the old churchyard stands a stately house in extensive grounds complete with a lake, where the lord of the manor resided but which is now an hotel.

The mill near the moor in Flitwick

Irrespective of all the building, Flitwick still treasures its moor, a nature reserve managed by the Beds & Hunts Naturalist Trust. Many years ago spring water from the moor was bottled and sold for its iron content, and the commoners were allowed to dig the peat for their fires. On one side of the moor is the mill, powered by water from a tributary of the river Flitt. Mallards and Muscovey ducks live along the banks, visiting adjoining properties daily for titbits and nesting behind convenient bushes. The lane between the mill and moor floods, and then the story is retold of the night it flooded to a great depth and the occupants of a carriage and the horses pulling it were all drowned.

⌘ GRAVENHURST

Upper and Lower Gravenhurst were once known as Over and Nether Gravenhurst.

Many changes have taken place this century. Men worked very hard in the fields, taking the Bedfordshire Clanger to eat cold. This was a suet dumpling with meat, potatoes and onion at one end and jam at the other. One father of seven children was allowed to eat everything but the meat, which he took home for his wife to make another dumpling. On the third day he was allowed to consume all.

Men were also employed at the kiln at Lower Gravenhurst making bricks. The clay was drawn out of the pit by the water mill. Bricks were dried out under thatched barns and used for local houses. Some of the first bricks made can be seen in a house behind Upper Gravenhurst church. The clay pit is now a lake and is used for private fishing. It is reputed that a young girl drowned herself in the pit after losing her baby and that her ghost has been seen in a nearby house.

Probably the oldest house in the village is 'Little Ion'. Originally mentioned in the Domesday Book as one house, it was divided into four cottages for the Ion Farm workers. One family was rife with fleas and when they vacated their cottage it was fumigated; sulphur candles were placed in an upstairs room and as they burnt low they set fire to the oak beams below and caused a fire. 'Little Ion' was then made once more into a single home in the 1950s and has been beautifully restored.

In the 19th century the population was larger at Lower Gravenhurst and there were seven or eight fountains of icy cold spring water, but when running water was laid on all the fountains ran dry. Flush toilets had arrived! What joy to the young lady who once paid a visit to the bottom of the garden late at night and promptly sat on a chicken sheltering on the toilet seat.

Chestnut Tree House was formerly one of the three public houses in the village and also served at a later date as a post office. At one time people would walk down to the Old Mill to pick up their freshly ground flour. Fresh bread was collected from a bakery near St Giles' church.

St Giles' is still used and local weddings are always an attraction. The tiny church of St Mary at Lower Gravenhurst is now redundant but the marks of bullets and bayonets can still be seen on the door, a legacy from the Civil War. It is also rumoured that a row of 17th century cottages on the Campton road was used as a hospital during this war.

⌘ GREAT BARFORD

There has been a settlement here for at least a thousand years. Great Barford is well situated by the river Great Ouse and navigation is possible to the Wash and the North Sea. Until the Second World War, there were 700 to 800 inhabitants with none of the modern essentials such as piped water, gas, electricity and mains drainage. The chief employment was in agriculture; women and men worked in the fields, and after the harvest the children would accompany their mothers and go gleaning. The school bell had great significance for the village, it acted as the farmworkers' clock. It rang in the morning and again after the dinner break.

Sheep were driven to the river once a year to be dipped and washed before being clipped; this caused great commotion. Cows walked through the village twice a day and caused deep ruts on the then dirt roads. There were ten shops and six public houses at one time. The Manning Fair had winter quarters at what is now Fairway. The elephants on their walks always rubbed their backs against the cottage wall nearby and the cry would go out for people to push against the wall on the other side as it was feared the wall would be knocked down.

Poachers were known to throw a couple of rabbits over the policeman's garden gate so that he would turn a blind eye to their misdeeds.

The river Ouse at Great Barford

Crops included parsley for drying purposes, sent to Scotland via Blunham railway station; rushes from the river were dried on what is now Pyms Close and sent to Burton-on-Trent, the brewing centre, for barrel packing.

Great Barford has changed with the times – there is still agriculture but now most people work outside the village.

⌘ HARLINGTON

Sheltered by the Chiltern Hills, Harlington at the turn of the century was a very small community whose inhabitants were mostly employed in farming, quarrying and on the railway. When Harlington was given a railway station neighbouring Toddington was the loser, for landowners haggled over settlement prices and now Toddington has a Station Road, but no station!

Harlington parish church is medieval, with commemorative stained glass windows depicting *The Pilgrim's Progress*. One famous vicar was William Spencer, also renowned as an artist who died in 1905. For many years his grave was 'lost' under rubbish in the cemetery, but in 1980, during clearing up operations, the grave reappeared with the word 'Resurgam' in view.

Next to the church stands the old school. For many years until the outbreak of the First World War schoolchildren were taught to make straw plait to be sold to the hat manufacturers of Luton. A horse-drawn carrier cart would collect the plait from several villages and take it to Luton for the early market each Monday. One Harlington schoolmistress prepared a scale of charges for the plait which was accepted throughout the whole area.

Harlington House, know as the Manor, stands at the crossroads behind old, red brick walls. It is a 16th century timber-framed building which has been extended over the years. Since approximately 1500, the Manor has been occupied by important families, including the Burwells, Wingates and Pearces. King Charles II is reputed to have slept there and John Bunyan was taken there after his arrest in neighbouring Samsell in 1660. Squire Frances Wingate JP ordered him to be taken to Bedford prison, where he wrote *The Pilgrim's Progress*.

The tercentenary of Bunyan's death, 1988, was marked in the village by the planting of an oak sapling beside the famous Bunyan's Oak (now dead), under which he is said to have preached many times.

Bury Orchard is a lovely piece of green parkland in the centre of the village, held in trust for the recreation of parishioners. It boasts a large pond called The Dell, formerly known as Bacchus Pond, an old excavation pit which has filled with water from many underground springs. During the summer months it is visited by moorhens and ducks, further enhancing this attractive feature.

A visit to Harlington would not be complete without a stroll along Barton Road with its panoramic views of Sundon Hills and Sharpenhoe Clappers, whilst from the bottom road can be seen a quaint line of houses of all shapes and sizes outlined against the sky.

⌘ HARROLD

Estate agents describe Harrold as 'a much sought after village' and indeed it is a very pleasant and attractive place. It has the river, crossed by a 13th century bridge, which is a little like the shoemaker's hundred year old knife which had had six new blades and four new handles – the bridge has been repaired so many times that perhaps only the location and design of the original have remained! It has a beautiful church, some parts of which date from the 13th century, a village green set with lime trees, beneath which stand a 17th century butter market and a lock-up. Also there are many stone houses and cottages.

One resident remembers that the houses used to have pumps in the yard and water had to be pumped up to the tank before it could be drawn from the taps. As a lad he used to earn 6d a week going to one house every day to pump up.

The ancient industry of the village was wool but in latter times leather took over and there were four factories engaged in dressing and finishing hides, which were imported, mostly from India. Now it is no longer economic to import skins and one by one the factories have closed. Years ago many of the village women supplemented their income by making pillow lace. Unhappily all the old lace

The lock-up at Harrold

makers have died or moved away, through there has been a revival of interest when evening classes have offered instruction.

Once a year the Pit Run is organised, so called because it is run round the country park which is on the site of the old gravel pits. When the park was made there was a suggestion to rename it 'the Park Run' but no one wanted that, so it remains 'the Pit Run' to the probable confusion of future contestants. If the weather is fine it is a beautiful route, starting from Harrold Green and running round the lakes to Odell and back. The park has a wealth of wildlife and many interesting birds on the water.

⌘ HAYNES

Set in mid-Bedfordshire, Haynes is situated between the A6 and the A600. The village boundaries extend far afield, which is perhaps why focal points are named Ends – Silver End, Northwood End, Church End and West End, the 'posh end' taking the name of Three Ways.

The 14th century church and Haynes Park Manor are steeped in history and

Haynes Park Manor

legend. The manor, once a boarding school for girls, dates back to 1564. In 1605 James I and Queen Anne stayed at the manor and attended a service at Haynes church on 30th July, this being the year of the Gunpowder Plot. Samuel Pepys in his diary mentions that Sir George Carteret bought the manor for his son in 1667.

The advowson of Haynes church was given to Chicksands Priory in 1150. The earliest surviving masonry is of the 14th century church, which is dedicated to St Mary. This was in association with the rise in popularity of the cult of the Virgin, which swept England in response to the Black Death. The church itself is the proud owner of the Cloth of Gold on which Queen Victoria knelt at her coronation. She bequeathed it to Lord Thynne, then the lord of the manor, who subsequently gave it to the church. It can be seen decorating the altar table during flower festivals and other special occasions.

At the south end of the village is a thickly wooded area called the Warren, where there is a private road overlooking green pastures sloping down to a brook. Barking deer as well as many other animals and birds have their homes in the Warren. The northern boundary of the village is flanked by a backcloth of beech woods, the fringe of Wilstead Hill, which gives a clear view to Bedford.

Haynes has original Elizabethan houses, thatched cottages and since the Second World War various 20th century homes. Many terraced cottages have been renovated, their owners taking great pride in recapturing the past while incorporating modern conveniences.

⌘ HEATH AND REACH

The village was formerly two hamlets but today it tends to merge into Leighton Buzzard in spite of vigorous efforts to keep its own identity. New estates have sprung up to replace fields and meadows, but there are still some lovely old timbered and thatched buildings left which give a flavour of life as it was. The pump-house, crowned with a clock-tower, remains a feature of the village green at the top of the hill.

In years gone by there was a village crier who walked the streets shouting news and ringing his bell for a shilling, and the sexton also used the church bells to announce the age of the departed as they were wheeled through the village in a glass-covered bier for all to see, whilst the children concentrated on counting the bell-tolls. Every blind was drawn.

Heath and Reach knew how to celebrate too. The annual village feast was held in November on the green, when Liza Hawkes would attract a fascinated crowd to see her make brown and cream striped rock. The flower and vegetable show was a dressier occasion, held at Baldry's field in the summer and followed by a cricket match for the men.

As a community, the village fared well. The three Miss Blewitts, the village's eccentric benefactresses, made sure the poor and needy were catered for, and each cottager paid a penny a week to the Nursing Association so that a nurse could live in the community and care for everyone. Only for rare emergencies was a doctor called in. When a baby was born, it always received a little gift from the village school, often in the form of a pretty paper ball, and the Mothers' Union traditionally gave a bonnet and a pair of bootees.

Sand remains the chief industry of Heath and Reach, silica a speciality, but no longer are local families the owners, nor do the pits provide a high level of employment since the advent of automation. Gone is the steady procession of horses and carts in the direction of Linslade canal, gone too the wheelwright's trade! Working the allotments used to be a necessary task, whereas many are overgrown nowadays, and the pea and potato picking and wood activities have also died out. Rug making has gone and lace making only survives as a minority hobby, when once the little girls all attended Saturday morning classes.

⌘ HENLOW

The name Henlow is believed to derive from Old English henna hlaw, 'hill frequented by wild birds', and was mentioned in the Domesday Book. The village is best known for RAF Henlow, first established in 1918 for the then new Royal Flying Corps.

Also well known is Henlow Grange, famous as a health farm and frequented by many showbusiness and sports personalities. Its most notable pre-war occupant was Alan Lennox-Boyd, who represented Mid-Bedfordshire in Parliament, later becoming Colonial Secretary and finally Lord Boyd of Merton. The gates leading to the pit recreation ground were erected in his memory and his family donated the Boyd Field (formerly known as Paddling Ditch Meadow) to the Scouts of the district. A much earlier occupant, in the 17th century, was a Richard Raynsford, reputed to be Chief Justice of the Kings Bench. Raynsford Lower School bears his name.

A peaceful scene near the river at Henlow

For several hundred years, the squire made contributions to the parish houses, schools and employment on the estate and farms. The majority of families depended in one way or another on the land and were very poor, often existing on a staple diet of turnips and potatoes and living in grossly overcrowded conditions, but they had great dignity and were generally most industrious. The main cottage industry was straw plaiting and quite young children had to do their share, often before going to school. This seems to have died out at the end of the 19th century. In medieval times Henlow was known for bowstring making.

On the famous voyage of the *Mayflower* were John Tilley, his wife Joan (nee Cooper) and daughter Elizabeth of this parish, which has led, through the Rev. Ashfold, a former vicar, to a link with the Pilgrim John Howland Society in Rhode Island, USA. Their members have twice made pilgrimages to the 12th century church of St Mary and have made generous donations including a pewter spoon, a replica of one carried on the *Mayflower*, now displayed in the church.

The church is in a beautiful setting on a rise above the Pit (formerly a gravel pit), with the village pump in the foreground and a horse trough built to commemorate Queen Victoria's Diamond Jubilee.

In 1819 Thomas Hare built a smock windmill, which had a revolving cap to turn the sails into the wind. Sadly, this fell into disrepair and was finally demolished when the flour mill was extended. This mill, believed to be one of the oldest working mills in Bedfordshire, is still owned by the Hare family and manufactures a range of malt flours.

⌘ HOCKLIFFE

The village of Hockliffe dates back to the 11th century, although there is some evidence of a settlement in Roman times. The name is derived from 'Hocga's cliff', the cliff referring to the hill on which the 14th century church was built.

The only other building of any importance was the Hospital of St John the Baptist, which stood on the site of what is now Hockliffe House. It was intended as a hospital for the destitute poor and had the dubious honour of having its own chapel and burial rights.

Since the original settlement round the church, Hockliffe has now spread down both sides of Watling Street, with the centre well away from the church. The emergence of Watling Street as a main highway between London and North Wales was the main reason for the development of Hockliffe as it is today. At one stage there were as many as 14 inns serving the traveller.

Hockliffe gained a nationwide reputation for the bad state of its road through the village and became widely known as Hockley in the Hole. The reason for the poor state was the vast number of cattle and sheep being driven through to the markets in London. In order to alleviate the problem, toll gates were installed at the junction of Church Lane and Watling Street and on both the Leighton Buzzard and Woburn roads. This must have improved the condition as Daniel Defoe mentioned in 1742:

> 'That the most dismal piece of ground for travelling that ever was in England has been handsomely repaired.'

One of the side results from the vast number of cattle being driven through was that by the early 17th century all of Hockliffe's fields were enclosed – a rarity in those days.

Considering the small number of inhabitants it is interesting to learn that during the early 1800s three other churches were opened. One was the Independent Congregational, which built its own church, a building which can still be seen. The Wesleyan Methodists opened a church in the building which was used in later years as the village hall, and the Primitive Methodist chapel used the original meeting house of the Congregationalists.

⌘ HOUGHTON REGIS

In Saxon times Houghton Regis was a very large parish. Its origins date back to Stone Age man and their flint weapons can still be picked up in the fields surrounding the village. It reduced in size considerably during medieval times but it has now grown enormously, though it still retains its village atmosphere.

Its name is Saxon; meaning 'settlement on a hill'; regis means 'of the king'. Houghton Regis is shown in the Domesday book as being a prosperous village with one of the largest populations for its size in the land – there were 240 people living there.

The manor house, now called Houghton Hall, is still in existence and well maintained, although it is currently used as offices. The original manor was built by Henry Brandreth, who was the lord of the manor of Houghton Regis, in 1652. His daughter, Alice, had the existing hall built in 1700 and it is said her ghost can be seen walking there. This family did a lot to stabilise Houghton Regis and the village owes them a great deal.

Another person who did much for the village is Thomas Whitehead. He established one of the earliest schools in England in Houghton Regis in the 17th century. Lessons originally began in the church, but when he died he bequeathed his home to the school and a proper school was built on his land facing the village green. Now this has been demolished, although the old school house is still there, and a modern school has been built behind the parish church. The church itself is Norman and boasts a beautiful font that is even older than the building.

The village green covers quite a large area and is situated in front of the old manor house. Soldiers were billeted on the green during the Second World War and in the past sheep grazed on it.

As the chalk in the ground at Houghton Regis produced white straw, which made it particularly good for making the hats for which the nearby town of Luton is renowned, at the end of the last century the people of Houghton Regis were able to make a very profitable living in the straw plaiting trade. Practically all the women were to be seen sitting outside their houses plaiting. The children, too, were employed. Indeed, plaiting schools were established, which caused a great deal of controversy as some of the children were undoubtedly exploited.

Later a cement works was established in Houghton Regis, again due to the large amount of chalk in the soil, and people moved into the area looking for work. The local people found a use for the coltsfoot plant that thrived in the chalk pits. They used to collect it and sell it to the local pharmacists for medicine.

Housing continues to be built, much of it on what was for centuries farmland. Fortunately, many of the old farmhouses remain and old buildings are being preserved.

⌘ HUSBORNE CRAWLEY

Husborne Crawley is a village of two settlements, Church End joined by School Lane to the Main End. It is in the latter that the greatest change has taken place. Until the 1960s almost all the houses in this part of the village were tied to the Duke of Bedford's estate, but since then these houses have been sold into private ownership.

Church End has changed very little and like most of the village is a conservation area and contains many listed buildings. One of these buildings is The Thatched Cottage, circa 1650. When first built it was owned by the local midwife, a single lady of dubious character. She added to her income by offering accommodation to journeymen, travellers, etc, when the local inns were full. Travelling highwaymen

Church End, Husborne Crawley

are known to have used this accommodation and legend has it that, to this day, some of their 'pickings' lie buried beneath three oak trees in the vicinity.

Although the village has no shops now, this has not always been the case. The bakery was the last shop to exist, and ceased baking about 1980. The dough was baked in coal heated ovens and resulted in delicious crusty loaves. Prior to the arrival of the electric cooker it was usual for the housewives of the village to mix their Christmas cake at home and take it to the baker to be baked at a cost of one penny. A post office was also run from the bakehouse.

In the 1920s a fruit shop was run from the building which now houses the ladies and gents toilets at the White Horse public house. This shop was later taken over by a butcher, and the slaughterer's wheel, which was used to pull up the carcases, can still be seen in one of the outhouses. During the war years a fresh fish shop was run from the premises by the landlord of the day

'That is as crooked as Crawley Brook' is a phrase which was often used, particularly to children when something, perhaps a row of stitching, was not as straight as it might have been. The brook has its source in Woburn and continues on its winding course until joining the Ousel near Moulsoe.

The Experimental Farm at Crawley Mill Farm was started in 1876 as a result of the Rothamsted Experiment. It was felt desirable to test whether the light, sandy soil of the Woburn area would produce similar results to those on the heavy soil at Rothamsted. There are grain samples at the farm dating from before 1900. Dr Harold Mann, who was world famous, was employed at the Experimental Farm before 1900, when he left to go to India, where he studied the tea plant. He was later invited to Russia to advise on the cultivation of tea.

⌘ KEMPSTON

Kempston lies below the river Ouse just west of Bedford. Angles, Saxons, Romans, Danes and Vikings each in their turn found it a convenient place to raid or settle, but the parish eventually shaped itself into 13 or so endships, or hamlets, centred on All Saints' church. The High Street became know as 'the Town' and gradually absorbed some of the Ends but continues to be regarded as part of the village by many.

The Out-Ends, unofficially called the 'Odd Ends', together with Church End now form 'Kempston Rural'. Wood End and West End are signposted, but for others names like Moor End House or Box End Road offer the only clues. Some have never been mapped at all, such as Crow End, Mill End and Howe End. The parish includes Kempston Hardwick and Gibraltar Corner, named after a cottage out on its own like the Rock.

Many memories of village life focus on the river, which used to be more accessible. There were basins of shallow water safe enough for learners with belts of twisted reeds under their arms. As fields were ploughed up for crops, particularly in the Second World War, access became less easy. Finally, even the river changed its character. The Water Board dredged the river bed to improve land drainage and suddenly the water became a fast-flowing current between steep banks. Backwaters turned into muddy ditches, landing stages and mooring posts were left high and dry. Fishing and canoeing can still be enjoyed, but not punting. Paddling is limited to a spot near the old mill.

The Keep, Kempston

Other landmarks still remembered have disappeared. At Green End there used to be a brickyard behind Kempston House. Some of the cottages are built with the bricks, which were handmade. Moist top-clay was moulded into shape, then stacked in rows under slanting covers to dry out before going into the kiln.

Two big private estates disappeared in Kempston's urban development, but both early 19th century houses remain. The Grange now stands in Addison Howard Park, graciously given to Kempston by the last owner in memory of a son killed in the First World War. The Manor has changed occupants many times since it was last a squire's home, yet the inevitable ghost legend survives in the story of the tragic return of a former owner and his lady from a Christmas Eve Ball. Their young son, awakened by the noise of the carriage, rushed out to greet them and was trampled to death by the horses. To this day, so the legend says, if you should venture down the drive late on Christmas Eve, you will hear the sound of the carriage, the neighing of the horses, and the screams of the boy as he meets his death!

Finally, mention must be made of the Barracks, a real local landmark since 1876. During the Second World War 40,000 men passed through its gates. All that remains now of its former glory is the Keep, happily retained as a social centre in the surrounding housing scheme.

⌘ KEYSOE

In the 11th century the name of the village was written as Caisot, Caissot or Chaisot. The pronunciation 'Kayso' can still be heard now and again.

Until 1870 Keysoe was one of the few villages to have a school. This was the National School, named because it was maintained by the National Society for the Propagation of the Gospel, a Church of England organisation. The building is one of the few of its kind still standing today.

Keysoe windmill was built in 1800 and was the last working post mill in Bedfordshire. In 1935 it was the only one where flour was still ground and dressed solely by windpower. The mill was blown down in a gale in 1947.

The nonconformist chapel at Brook End was built in 1741. John Bunyan is said to have preached at Keysoe in the surrounding woods and to have lodged at a local farmhouse. In 1808, Joel Miles dissented from this chapel to form Keysoe Row Baptist chapel, which still has the original hat pegs and oil lamps and is one of only two thatched chapels in Bedfordshire (Roxton has the other).

In North Bedfordshire, copies of pamphlets written by Annie Freeman can still be found, but in 1910, the news of the Keysoe Miracle was on the lips of many Christians. Annie was a weakly child until 12 years of age, when she grew stronger and went to work, but in 1887 she was ill with pleurisy and rheumatic fever. After several spells in hospital, she lost the use of her legs, was bedridden and was visited by 24 doctors. In 1909, she had a vision and was assured of a recovery, but not until

14th April 1910, when she heard a voice telling her to arise, did Annie get to her feet – fully recovered.

Another legend which may be true is that of a poor countryman called Matcham. During the time of the enclosures when life was hard for all but a few, Matcham was found guilty of sheep stealing and hanged from an elm tree, the stump of which can still be found at the corner of the field behind College Farm buildings. The story goes that if you approach this tree at twilight and say 'Matcham, Matcham, I've brought you some broth', a voice will be heard to reply, 'Cool it!'

⌘ KNOTTING

Knotting is one of the smaller villages in Bedfordshire, off the A6, some ten miles north of Bedford. The spelling of its name has been variously Chenotinga in the 11th century, Knottyngges in the 14th century and Knottinge in the 17th century.

Knotting church has a rare dedication to St Margaret of Antioch. Most of the fabric dates from the time of the Normans. Cock fighting took place in the chancel on Shrove Tuesday in 1634-6, when even the rector and churchwardens appear to have been present. The rector as a result lost his living. The unusual pulpit and sounding board are thought to be 17th century and the oak pews date from before the Reformation.

An old cottage behind the church is reputed to be haunted, but such tales are hard to confirm. Another story says there was once an illegal pub in the village!

Knotting remains much as it has been over the centuries – and a preservation order has been placed on the telephone box!

⌘ LIDLINGTON

Lidlington is a village to the south-west of Bedford, with easy access to the M1 motorway at Brogborough. It is positioned at the bottom of a steep winding hill, where an annual hill race is held on Spring Bank Holiday Monday. The outskirts of Lidlington are surrounded by grazing land and near the High Street are hills and woodlands providing pleasant walks.

In the past Lidlington has been connected with two Lord Mayors of London. One was born in the village in 1714. The other, Thomas Johnson, was befriended by a Lidlington family as a poor pack boy selling goods to country folk. When he was ill the family nursed him and when, in later years, he became a rich London merchant he did not forget them. He formed a charity to provide coal for old people and widows in the village, and also for helping apprentices buy tools. This charity is still going today and known as the Thomas Johnson Charity.

Lidlington belonged to various families until 1804, when the Duke of Bedford took it over and had several houses built for the local workforce. These houses had

The view from Lidlington Hill

no front doors and it has been said that this was because the Duke and Duchess hated to go past and see women gossiping on the doorstep!

The railway line opened in 1846 and was the main link with other villages, the only other transport being horse and cart. There were seven farm dwellings in the village which offered the main employment. The largest farm in the area was called Great Farm, having a total of 1,001 acres. This comprised 380 acres in the village and the remainder at Bury Ware Farm, at the top of the hill. Root and cereal crops were grown here and the lower land was used for rearing stock. Great Farm was owned by the Duke of Bedford and run as one farm until 1947, when the land at Bury Ware was sold.

Until 1935 only a few streets were established in the village. The High Street had a few houses including two pubs, the Red Lion and the Green Man. Church Street was cobbled and also had several houses. When Stewartby brickworks opened people began to move into the area for work. The Marston Valley brickworks were completed in 1935 and this provided even more employment. Council houses were built in Station Road to provide homes for the workmen and their families. Marston Valley were contracted by the Council to build more houses, and the village continued to expand.

Lidlington was a fairly self-sufficient village, with a bakehouse in Lombard Street, a post office and a general store, which sold everything, in Church Street. There was also a blacksmith and wheelwright, who made coffins for the villagers. Besides the two chapels in the village, the old St Margaret's church was built on a hill near the High Street. This site was abandoned in 1886 as the ground began to slip causing the church to crumble. A large new church was built on level ground soon after and can be seen today facing the churchyard on High Street.

⌘ LITTLE STAUGHTON

Little Staughton is a very ancient village. The name has changed from Stockton to Stokton and eventually to Staughton. But, as reported in the *Bedfordshire Magazine* dated 1948, Little Staughton was known as the 'Lost Village', due to the fact that, during the Second World War, the top end of the village was demolished to make way for the aerodrome. This included 20 houses and two public houses, namely the Bushel and Strike and the Shoulder of Mutton.

The aerodrome was used for Flying Fortresses and Lancaster Bombers. Many lives were lost in bombing raids from Little Staughton airfield. One day, a Lancaster Bomber took off from the short runway and one of its wheels caught the roof of the Baptist chapel and tore a great hole. As a result of this, and much to the dismay of the whole village, the chapel had to be demolished. The chapel had been built in the 17th and 18th centuries and was a very beautiful building with a gallery upstairs running its whole length. Eventually, in 1957, a new chapel was built in the centre of the village.

The church is early 13th century. It used to be called St Margaret's but is now All Saints'. Standing in a very prominent position, it has the most commanding views of the surrounding countryside; the spires of five other churches can be sighted on a clear day. In 1900 the church spire was struck by lightning, and, on 2nd August 1906, the village suffered a phenomenal storm, when crops and vegetables were torn to shreds by giant hailstones. Over 400 window panes were broken and a field of onions was so badly damaged that the smell of onions hung over the village for several days.

As in many of the villages, lace making was what the womenfolk did to earn a little money to live on, and there was once a lace school in Little Staughton. The men often had to be away from home for weeks at a time, mowing hay perhaps, or doing drainage work to make a living.

There are some tales of witchcraft and murder in Little Staughton. In October 1653, a certain Emma Saunders was accused of bewitching William Holland. In 1870, a murder was committed in Little Staughton by William Bull, who was 21 years of age. The old lady he murdered was Sarah Marshall, who lived almost opposite the local shop, in an old cottage. Bull was executed in Bedford on 3rd April 1871.

In common with other villages, Little Staughton has changed tremendously over recent years and many new houses have been built. There used to be four public houses; now only the Crown remains. It was completely gutted by a fire on 14th February 1972 and the chimney stack was the only part left standing. In 1973 the new Crown was opened on the site of the old inn, the old chimney stack having been incorporated into the new building.

Moreteyne Manor, Marston Moreteyne

⌘ MARSTON MORETEYNE

Life in this village has changed greatly in the last 60 or so years. The village shop has gone, public houses have been converted into private homes and many fields have been lost. Blacksmith's Row is still there though. The old village blacksmith's shop was at the end of a row of terraced cottages (they still remain the same).

In this village is the stone connected with a local tradition of a visit from the Devil. The story is that the Devil, with a former owner of the field in which the stone is situated, was playing jumps on the Sabbath. He took a leap from the church tower, and alighting on the stone jumped with the offending party into eternity. That part of the village is still known as 'The Jumps'.

The Snagge family have always had a strong connection with the village. Their family tomb is inside the church. John Snagge, the famous radio and BBC commentator, was lord of the manor. The old Manor Farm (famous for its surrounding moat) has been converted and is now Moreteyne Manor Restaurant, taking its name from a very old family of the village.

⌘ MAULDEN

Maulden stands on the Greensand ridge, approximately one mile east of Ampthill. It is a long development with several Ends. Maulden is believed to mean 'hill marked with a cross'.

The village's origins are not known but Roman remains have been found to the south of the village. It was mentioned in the Domesday Book, where it was spelled 'Meldone'.

The hill is still marked with a cross in the shape of the church, which keeps a watchful eye over the village, although little of the original stands today. The north wall dates from the 12th century and the tower from the 14th. Changes large and small have taken placed over the centuries. In 1858 the church was largely rebuilt to accommodate a growing population. At the beginning of the last century, the roof was repaired and a new organ and heating system were installed.

North of the church stands a strange, octagonal building, the Ailesbury Mausoleum. Built of sandstone, it is entered by a stairway between the buildings. It was erected in 1656 by Thomas, Earl of Elgin in memory of his wife, Diana, Countess of Oxford and Elgin, who had died in 1654. Underneath is a large vaulted crypt, with 27 niches for bodies, which shows signs of dating back to Norman times and may once have been a meeting place connected to the old church.

As in many villages, the church, manor and rectory were situated close together, each with a moat. The manor has long since disappeared but is believe to have stood north of the church in a field called the Grove or Grovebury.

The old rectory, however, still stands, on a second hill to the east of the church. It probably dates back to the 16th century. At the time of the enclosures, the rector gained possession of the land immediately surrounding the house and around 1797 the gardens are thought to have been landscaped by Capability Brown himself. The house and grounds were sold by the diocese in 1936 and the property has since been known as Maulden Grange.

One rector to make a great impact on the village was the Reverend Charles Ward, who survived two wives and worked tirelessly in the parish for over 50 years. In particular, he was instrumental in establishing the school. He raised the money for a National School in 1849. His wife and daughter helped with the teaching and he worked towards the erection of the present building, although he died before its completion.

Once Maulden was largely self sufficient. The fertile land made agriculture, especially market gardening, one of the main sources of employment. The community was greatly affected by the Enclosure movement, which, while increasing efficiency, also caused loss of livelihood and great hardship. Records show that the military had to be called out in Maulden to prevent a riot.

Proximity to the Luton hat industry encouraged straw plaiting. There was a plaiting school in the village in the 19th century. Lace making was also an important occupation. At Green End there was a sandstone quarry which provided building materials and at Water End there was a mill.

Not surprisingly, ghost stories abound, from the monks who cross New Road, to the boy in a Tudor ruff who plays mischievous pranks in one of the village's newer houses. A ghostly pony drags chains up and down Streets Hill on

Silsoe Road and a middle aged 'gentleman' follows people down one of the village footpaths!

⌘ MELCHBOURNE

Melchbourne is a small village in the north-western corner of Bedfordshire, five miles from Rushden and about twelve miles from Bedford. The main part of the village is up a no-through-road – Park Road – which leads to the church and to the large mansion house that overlooks the whole village.

The surrounding countryside is undulating and very pretty. It is a good mix of arable and pasture land. Many hedges have been retained and there are some lovely woods, which are constantly maintained and managed, with new trees being planted at regular intervals. On the outskirts of the village the Oakley Hunt have their kennels, where the hounds are kept. It is quite a sight in the winter month to see the Hunt 'tally-ho' across the fields.

Melchbourne is steeped in history. It is mentioned in the Domesday Book and it was a site of the Knights Hospitallers. They probably built the first church on the present site. The existing church of St Mary Magdalene is a Grade 1 listed building. The foundations and tower remain medieval. The church was remodelled in the 18th century and is now one of the largest churches in North Bedfordshire.

The mansion house was originally built by Lord St John of Bletsoe, who bought the manor of Melchbourne from Edward, Earl of Bedford, in 1620. There are traces of the 17th century farmhouse in the existing house, but it has been altered and modernised over the centuries. The house stayed in the St John family up until 1930. They built the school in Melchbourne in 1870 (it is now converted into a private house). They also built (or allowed to be built!) the local pub, hence its name: the St John Arms. The family shield can be seen on both these buildings. It has been said that the pub is a long way from the centre

Melchbourne Park mansion

of the village because the St Johns at the time did not want 'drunken' villagers near their own home!

The mansion and estate were sold in 1930. The mansion was kept as a family home up until the late 1970s, it was then sold to a property developer and converted into several apartments. There is a very large village hall that was rebuilt by American servicemen during the Second World War, when they were based at the mansion.

⌘ MILLBROOK

The name Millbrook means just that, as there used to be a mill just outside the village which was destroyed around two centuries ago.

The whole village used to belong to the Duke of Bedford, the cottages all being tenanted by farm workers. Cottages and gardens alike were regularly inspected and woe betide anyone with a weed in sight! Most of the cottages are over a hundred years old. The villagers were known for their pillow lace making and also straw plaiting, and the highlight of the year was the annual visit of the fair.

The village is traditionally associated with *The Pilgrim's Progress*; the wooded valley near the church is reputed to be Bunyan's 'Valley of the Shadow of Death'. Another literary association is with the poet Milton, who is said to have planted the mulberry tree in the rectory garden which is still there today. There used to be a blacksmith and Saxon pottery on this site. Close to the rectory is a natural spring from which villagers used to fetch their water. This is called the Boiling Pot because the water is always turbulent.

The main focal point is the church, which stands 363 feet above sea level. Built in the 13th century but extensively restored in the 19th, it still has part of its original structure. In the church are the tombs of Lord and Lady Holland, who lived in Ampthill Park House but had strong connections with Millbrook.

The village hall was originally two cottages. These were knocked into one and given by the Duke of Bedford to the villagers as a reading room.

There are supposed to be several ghosts in the area. One is an invisible horseman known as Galloping Dick, who can sometimes be heard, but not seen, descending Millbrook Hill. This rogue used to hold up stagecoaches on the Woburn road. Another is a headless spectre who is said to haunt the vicinity of Millbrook Station.

⌘ MILTON BRYAN & BATTLESDEN

The villages of Milton Bryan and Battlesden are so small that if you blink while passing through you might miss them. But they do have, and have had, a few memorable moments and people. St Peter's church at Milton Bryan has a stained glass window donated by the widow of Sir Joseph Paxton, the gardener and architect, who lived here as a boy. He designed a stately mansion in the style of a French chateau, which stood at Battlesden, but sadly is now demolished. Battlesden boasts a 13th century church.

A part of village life now completely gone from Milton Bryan is the wooden chapel that stood on the edge of the village pond for nearly 130 years. None of the landowners would let the Methodists have a piece of land to build a chapel, so they purchased materials with the help of Dunstable friends and the little wooden chapel was built in sections and brought from Dunstable in the dead of night and erected, partly over the village pond. For many years their hymn singing could be heard every Sunday.

The Red Lion public house was originally a farm and dairy. The lady of the manor, a Miss Synot, owned it at one time, allowing it to be used as a hostelry. It was never open on a Sunday, and closed at 9.30 pm during the week. The locals would sneak in the back door so they could still get their jug of ale. Spirits were not sold but could be got from the manor house for medicinal purposes. It has changed a great deal since then!

The large row of thatched cottages opposite the pub was once a coaching inn. For many years afterwards cobblestones would rise from the ground when the occupiers were digging their potatoes. The cobbles led to the end of the garden, where the horses were stabled. The building is over 500 years old and has seen many families come and go.

Milton Bryan – Sir Joseph Paxton's birthplace

There is a building at the north end of the village which was purpose built for use during the Second World War as a radio station. Its aim was to send false messages, wrong instructions and propaganda to demoralise the Nazis. It is understood that Sir Winston Churchill often visited it.

Mag's Lane, one of the four exit roads from Milton Bryan, supposedly got its name from Mag the ghost, who walks at the dead of night. Many reports from villagers (not all of them after the pub was shut) have come forth over the years of actual sightings and of the cold and misty aura that comes along at certain times, sending shivers up the spine and feet hurrying home.

⌘ MILTON ERNEST

Milton Ernest has the unusual distinction of being bisected by a thoroughfare originally used for driving animals to market, now part of the A6, being on the river Ouse, and having the old London, Midland and Scottish Railway close by.

The oldest complete buildings, constructed during the 17th century, were thatched and built of stone brought down the river from Pavenham. They included several farms, barns and agricultural workers' cottages, most still in use. A section of the old bakehouse dates back to the 14th century.

Milton Hall, designed by Williams Butterfield for the Starey family in the 19th century, was a family home, replacing a gentleman's house built in 1660. Whilst Lord and Lady Ampthill were in residence, during the First World War, two royal princes, sons of King George V and Queen Mary, stayed there and could be seen rushing around the grounds on their bicycles. It was put to a very different use during the Second World War: as USAF Communications HQ which included amongst its residents Glenn Miller, the famous band leader.

Kennels of the Oakley Hunt were in the village from the 1830s until the 1970s, when they were moved to Melchbourne. A famous Master of the Hunt was Captain Arkwright, who bred the brown patches into hounds' coats, previously black and white.

Every villages has its unique features and surely one of the most unusual engineering feats locally must have been the removal of the water tower at the top of the hill. During the 1950s this was moved bodily for some distance using rollers. Much local and even national interest was generated.

Items of a more domestic nature peculiar to this village included an old charity started by Susannah Rolt in 1726 to give twelve twopenny loaves to the poor of the parish every Sunday. There are photographs of choirboys early last century bursting down the church paths with loaves in their hands for distribution. They often enjoyed a sweet given by the grateful recipients!

Another well appreciated effort at that time was the loan of baby clothes hampers by the vicar for six weeks to new born babies. There were three sets of varying value, issued according to the condition in which the previous loan had been returned. With the large families of those days, there would have been plenty of opportunity to judge!

As with most villages which were once self sufficient, there were many more tradespeople based and working in Milton Ernest, now only a handful. Before the First World War there was a staggering number of nearly 30 trades and crafts represented. They included a higgler. He was a breaker of rough stones to form the surface of roads, including the present A6! The agricultural thresher and his team from Milton Ernest used to go round to farms in quite a wide radius. Sadly the post office has closed but other bulwarks of village life remain.

⌘ NORTHILL & ICKWELL

The centre of Northill village, with the church, pond and green, is a pleasant sight. To the south is Ickwell, with a large village green, dwellings of various periods and Ickwell Bury in the parkland nearby.

The church of St Mary the Virgin, dominating the Northill scene, is of mainly ironstone construction and was commenced about 1330. The earliest recorded rector of the parish is Richard De Loda, in 1224. The Trailly family was patron of the living in the 13th century, but it later passed to the Crown. In 1620 the rectory and the advowson was purchased by the Worshipful Company of Grocers, with money bequeathed in the will of Dame Margaret Slaney. This patronage has continued to the present day.

The existence of a chantry college, associated with the church and founded in 1404, can only be identified by various fishponds and field names, such as College Pond Field, College Wood and College Meadow. The college was dissolved in 1547.

There are a number of interesting buildings of various periods close by, including Well Cottage, Cowhovel Row, The Grange, and Red Clapboard House, several sympathetically restored cottages and the old Methodist chapel in Sand Lane.

The largest group of buildings in Ickwell includes Ickwell Bury, a former mansion, which became a boarding school for boys prior to being severely damaged by fire in 1937. The original buildings dating from 1683 included the house, stables and barns surrounding a courtyard. Now owned by the Harpur Trust, the house is a residential centre of the Yoga for Health Foundation. A large, well-preserved dovecote is to be found in the grounds.

The Old House, on Ickwell green, is of medieval origin and is still partially surrounded by a moat. The grounds are occasionally open to the public. Tompion's Cottage, on the corner of the green, bears a plaque as the birthplace of the famous 17th century clockmaker. A clock dated 1683, above the stable block in Ickwell Bury, is said to be by Thomas Tompion.

Northhill's village green

The Club Room nearby, formerly the Ickwell Boys and Girls Club, given by the local squire, was originally a wheelwright's work-shop. Now used as a small public hall, run by trustees, it houses a thriving playgroup, so it is still fulfilling its designated purpose. The old smithy on the green is now used as changing rooms by the local football club.

There is little evidence of Roman occupation, save the scattering of coins distributed throughout the parish. As part of the Wixhamtree Hundred, it is thought that the Hundred meet was held at Deadman's Oak, now the road junction at the south end of Sheerhatch Wood.

The countryside surrounding the two villages is mainly agricultural, but contains a number of well-wooded areas. The Greensand Ridge Walk traverses the parish and there are many well-signposted public footpaths. Within easy walking distance is the Shuttleworth Collection of vintage aeroplanes, and the nearby Swiss Garden.

Although known to have been continuously inhabited for over 1,000 years, Northill has developed and grown at a fairly leisurely pace. Two large Conservation Areas, designated by the local authority, contain the more historically important features, including many listed buildings. The quiet charm of the peaceful village atmosphere has been largely undisturbed by the more intrusive aspects of the 21st century.

⌘ ODELL

In Saxon days the village was known as 'Woad Hill' because of the amount of woad growing in the area. A Saxon stronghold stood on the banks of the river and when this fell to the Normans the land was granted to Walter the Fleming, who promptly started to erect a motte and bailey castle. By Tudor times the 2,902 acre estate was in ruins. Through marriage it had come into the Chetwood family and in the 17th century was leased to William Alston, who, after much restoration work, bought the entire estate in 1633. The Alston family was still in residence in February 1931 when fire gutted the building, and the property was bought by the Lawson-Johnston family. In nearly 1,000 years only three families have held title to this estate – quite a record.

On the neighbouring hill stands the 15th century church with its Perpendicular tower. Records show that a church has stood here since 1200 at least, and many worthy names appear on the list of incumbents, including one Sir Oswald Butler, who was made to pay public penance for the sin of marrying! There was also John Bulkeley, a dissident priest unable to come to terms with the modern church, who found it politic to flee, together with family and friends, to the New World, where the settlement they founded grew to become the modern town of Concord, Massachusetts.

Odell is a tranquil place today and it is hard to imagine the pocket handkerchief village green being the site of a thriving market large enough to rival that at Olney. A horse fair was also held regularly and on these market days, by merely displaying a green bough by the door, the villagers claimed their right to sell beer without licence. This happy practice of 'tapping', however, was stopped in 1858.

Odell has always lived off the land – a farming community which until the middle of the 18th century farmed on a communal basis, when each winter the enormous village plough would be brought out and yoked with teams of both men and horses! Women would eke out a meagre living sitting by their doors making pillow lace or plaiting rushes.

Above the village is Odell Great Wood, once part of a vast forest stretching to the Fens. Not so large today, Odell Great Wood is still a haven for wild flowers,

The riverside at Odell

which, in their season, carpet the ground in primroses and bluebells, providing a beautiful walk for those prepared to climb the hill. This vantage point gives an excellent view of the river winding its way through the village, past the ancient mill with its waterwheel, where in olden days the local lord demanded 100 eels a year for rental. Fishing is still popular in Odell, both from the river bank and in the Country Park. Originating as gravel pits when the heart was torn out of the land to help build Milton Keynes, time and nature have healed the wounds and the Country Park is now a popular playground for the county. The lakes are also popular with waterfowl. There are so many geese today that conversation has to stop when they fly overhead on their way to and from their feeding grounds.

Tradition holds that Odell is haunted by Sir Rowland Alston, who sold his soul to the Devil. When the Devil came to collect his dues Sir Rowland fled in terror to the church and the Devil, seizing the church by the tower, shook the building in his rage and, it is said, left his fingermarks in the stonework of the southern jamb of the west door. Recently, an over-zealous builder carrying out maintenance work removed these 'offending' marks. However, once in every hundred years the ghost of Sir Rowland repeats that last frantic ride to avoid the Devil, and his next desperate gallop through the village is due in 2044.

⌘ OLD WARDEN

Although only a very small village Old Warden has several well-known features – the Shuttleworth Agricultural College and the Shuttleworth Collection of historic aircraft, which were set up as a trust by the late Mrs Shuttleworth as a memorial to her son Richard. The church dates from the early 12th century and is best known for its oak carvings collected by Lord Ongley in 1841 from Belgium, France and

The world famous Shuttleworth Collection is at Old Warden

Italy. It also contains medieval stained glass which came from Warden Abbey, itself famous for the Warden Pear. Many of the cottages, dating back to 1830–1850, are thatched and have fancy chimney pots.

The Swiss Garden is another feature of Old Warden and part of the village is on the Greensand Ridge Walk, which attracts numerous visitors.

⌘ PAVENHAM

The river Great Ouse flows around three sides of the high ground forming the village and parish of Pavenham. The river provided the rushes which fed the mat making industry at which generations of Pavenham men have toiled, while their womenfolk were busy at the lace pillows. Pavenham mats were once used on the floors of the Palace of Westminster. Baskets and other domestic articles are still made here from Pavenham rushes.

The centre of the village is dominated by the long and winding main street. Many of the stone-built cottages lining the street are snuggled under their cosy thatch, including the barn where John Bunyan preached.

The medieval church, dedicated to St Peter, stands on a hill above the village. Inside, it was panelled during the mid 1800s with Jacobean woodwork taken from the old Bury mansion during its rebuilding.

Church Lane itself was reputed to be haunted by the ghost of a Cavalier who had been waylaid by a group from the village – this was Roundhead territory. This unfortunate man was said to have tried to escape by jumping his horse over a gate at the top of the lane. His horse clipped the gate, throwing its rider, who was then killed and his body dumped in a nearby well. 'To this day', the story goes, no gate can be expected to remain long before collapsing in that particular gateway.

Pavenham is unusual in that a large number of the small cottages have been owner occupied for many years. The opportunity to buy occurred when the Bury estate came on the market in 1910. However, the earlier influence of the 'big house' could still be seen. In spite of the three public houses once in the village – the Swan, the Cock and the George and Dragon – great efforts

Stone-built houses line Pavenham's main street

had been made by the teetotal squire to provide alternative warm and congenial evening accommodation. A tea room and reading room were set up in a cottage previously used as the school rooms at the time a new village school was provided by the same benefactor.

Pavenham has changed in many ways. Much of it would still be recognisable to that ghostly Cavalier, but there are whole sections which would be new to him: the houses in Close Road and those built behind the belt of trees on the old Bury Park when the big house was finally pulled down. The barns of old College Farm, (Trinity College, Cambridge once owned the great tithes) are now converted into homes. But Pavenham is still Pavenham, and justly deserves the accolade, given to it by Arthur Mee, who said that Pavenham's long winding street with its stone houses is one of the most pleasing in the county of Bedfordshire.

⌘ PERTENHALL

Pertenhall has but little of fine buildings and few great men and no tales of high drama. The land is its past and present. Ask a farmer's man how he would describe the land here and back will come the answer, clear and precise – 'Heavy.' The old farmers called it 'four horse land', for that was the power needed to plough a single furrow. Today, hundreds of horses lurk in the engines of the modern tractors and the plough can cut seven deep furrows at a time. But still the caterpillar tractor rears up as the following plough sinks into the very wet ground.

Progress was slow, steady and hard won, developing a sturdy kind of man and woman, who had to work very hard to earn a living and develop self sufficiency. Perhaps that very hard way of life produced the peacefulness of the modern village; life was too hard for quarrelling; co-operation was a necessity.

In the 11th century the whole area was wooded, and in 1614 there were still 10 acres of woodland. Now alas only a vestige remains and the name Wood End to remind us of those former times. The same 1614 report shows the rest as mainly grass with a little arable. Now only a tiny percentage of grass remains and hedges have gone to make large fields suitable for the giant machines.

Pertenhall's 1,600 acres are well watered, both by the brook which flows through the village to join the river Kim and by numerous wells. The best known of these is Chadwell, bubbling away still, and renowned in medieval times for eyehealing properties and in more recent times for the cresses that grew abundantly there. The pump at Chapel Yard still stands close by the well that fed it. Broken now, it serves as a nesting place for tomtits and a reminder of the days when the ladies gathered with their buckets and gossiped together.

The great floral diversity of earlier times has gone with the increased use of plough and fertiliser. But bluebells and dog's mercury thrive in the hedges still, another relic of the ancient woodlands, and cowslips are returning thanks to a more enlightened verge cutting policy. Great patches of comfrey, pink, blue and white, thrive in the ditches and banks and quite hide the brook where the bridges span over. Some poppies survive in the unsprayed headlands and meadow orchids have reappeared in the chapel graveyard. Foxes are sometimes seen in the fields and periodically chased by the huntsmen. Partridge and pheasant are abundant, again targets for the hunter. Occasionally a muntjac deer is seen. Herons fly over from Grafham, fishing the streams and ponds.

⌘ PODINGTON, HINWICK & FARNDISH

Podington and the adjacent hamlets of Hinwick and Farndish are among the few lovely old places in North Bedfordshire to remain undeveloped and unspoilt. Despite their proximity to the industrial towns of Northants, the wide expanse of open fields surrounding them gives the feeling of being in the countryside, miles from anywhere. One of Podington's many attractive features is the High Street with the 13th century church and stone thatched cottages built in the early 1700s, where the womenfolk sat outside their door on summer evenings making pillow lace. Legend has it that lace making in Podington dates from Catherine of Aragon's incarceration in Kimbolton Castle and that Oak Cottage, where there was a lace making school, has a ghost – a lady in a lace bonnet looking for her bobbins.

Inevitably the way of life has changed with the times. Agriculture remains the main industry but no longer the main source of employment. Men and horses have

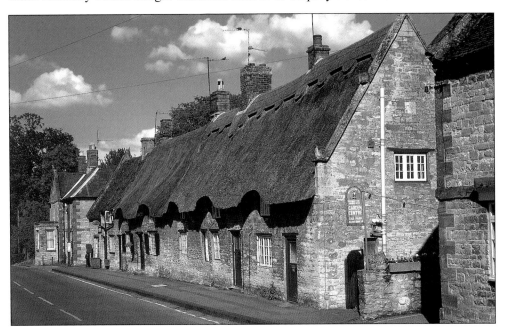

The old world charm of Podington

been replaced by machines. The activity once around the woodyard and brickyard, the wheelwright's and blacksmith's shops – all long since gone – is replaced by the comings and goings of modern farm machinery and the constant stream of traffic passing through.

Among the things which have survived through the years are the old Podington and Hinwick family names, and as long as there are Bryans, Gilberts, Normans, Orlebars, Pettits, Tompkins, Wildmans and descendants of the Browns the tales of bygone days will never die. The Cricket Club, well over 100 years old, tells the story of the occasion when the middle stump was knocked down leaving the outside stumps standing with the bails intact. It is perpetuated on the badge of its tie.

Podington and Hinwick appear in the Domesday Book, and evidence of Roman habitation was found in a field near the village and the footpath to Farndish. It is not insignificant that three miles across the fields is the old Roman town, known today as Irchester.

One cannot visit Podington and Hinwick without going to Farndish to see the tiny 11th century church with its squat tower and Saxon doorway. Reputed to be one of the smallest churches in the country, it stands on a grassy knoll, like an architectural gem.

⌘ POTTON

The long established and lively community of Potton, situated on the borders of Bedfordshire and Cambridgeshire, has been described as an 'outstanding conservation area of architectural and historic interest'. The market place is an excellent example of an enclosed medieval square, surrounded by styles ranging from the 16th century to the present day.

A tanyard, an agricultural engineering company, several mills and coprolite extraction no longer exist, but arable farming and market gardening, which have taken place for centuries, continue to a lesser degree.

Potton's centre

Countess Judith, niece of William the Conqueror, held Potton at the time of the Domesday survey. Between 1094 and 1271, the land was divided into four manors. By 1608 the Burgoyne family at Sutton were in possession, but little was retained by the 18th century. Admiral Lord Byng became lord of the manor in 1752, but after he had been condemned to death and shot for neglecting his duty on his own quarter deck in 1757, the land was inherited by the Torringtons of Southill. The fourth Viscount sold his estates to Samuel Whitbread in 1795. This family continued as lords of the manor until 1917, when their land and properties were purchased by many individuals.

Malcolm Stewart bought 713 acres of land in 1934 for the purpose of creating a Land Settlement Association. Unemployed men from the North were established on smallholdings, but few persisted. The Ministry of Agriculture took over the LSA during the Second World War and in 1983 offered the tenants the right to buy, vacant lots being put on the open market.

In 1203 market day was changed from Sunday to Saturday and continued until the late 19th century. Butchers rented stalls in the Shambles and people came from surrounding villages with eggs, butter, straw plait and pillow lace. Four yearly fairs were confirmed to Richard Burgoyne in 1670, the first, in January, becoming the well-known Horse Fair, held until the 1930s. The September Statute Fair, originally for the hiring of labour, developed into an annual 'merry making'. A Sheep Fair took place in October; 1,000 animals were on sale in 1821.

Pottonians have always met in the Square for organised celebrations, among them some less than peaceable assemblies. John Wesley, on his first visit, referred to the people of Potton as being 'wild beasts in abundance'. On 15th July 1832 'all the mob of Potton made a great riot to celebrate the passing of the Reform Bill'.

The Trade Directory for 1832 states that a weekly wagon left the Green Man for London, and in 1847 a weekly omnibus left the Swan for Smithfield. Fifteen inns were listed in the rate document of 1815, but by 1903 the number had risen to 32. Today there are fewer!

St Mary's church occupies a commanding position to the east. The present building appears to be 13th century. Special permission was obtained in 1802 for the building of the Baptist chapel. The Methodist church opened in 1840 and the Congregational chapel (now the United Reformed Church) in 1848. The Methodist church, closed in 1974, was sold to the Salvation Army.

⌘ PULLOXHILL

Pulloxhill is the modern name. Long ago the place was known as 'Pulloc's hill'. In the Domesday Book the name is spelt Polochessele.

The village is a very quiet, pretty and unspoilt place between two beautiful valleys. St James' church was dedicated in 1219 by Robert of Lismore. However, in 1846 the church, after falling into a ruinous condition, was taken down brick by brick and carefully rebuilt. Against the north wall of the chancel is a monument to Sir William Briers, 1653, who at one time owned the manor of Upbury, and his two wives Anne (Duckett) and Arabella (Crofts).

Pulloxhill has two interesting field names. Gold Close is so called because in

1680 gold quartz was dug up there. Because of an ancient law which states that all gold found in the UK is the property of the Crown, Charles II seized the ground and leased it to a firm of refiners. They discovered, after finding such small quantities that it did not even cover the cost of refining, that it was in fact a few flakes of mica in drifted stones.

The other field is called Bunions Hill. Some say it refers to the land held here by the Bunion family in the 13th century. Others say that John Bunyan the writer and preacher was on his way to preach at Lower Sanshill, which lies between Portobello Farm and Sharpenhoe Clappers, but before reaching his destination he was arrested on the hill and taken before the magistrate at Harlington next day.

Opposite the vicarage in the fields going towards Greenfields Hermitage Farm is the burial ground of the Quakers, which was in use for at least 50 years with three known burials there in the 18th century. Pulloxhill was a Quaker stronghold in the days of John Bunyan.

In 1596 Elizabeth Cole was hanged in Bedford for practising witchcraft in the village. In more recent years there has been a witch who always used to wear a long black dress. She lived by the village pond on the green. It is said she put a curse, by placing a toad in a jar of water and saying a few magic words, on a woman who gave out outwork of straw plaiting because she would not give her work to do. The straw plait woman lived where Whinnets Way is now situated. She was struck down by illness until the work was forthcoming, when she immediately recovered.

In the 14th century there were fullers (cleaners and thickeners of cloth) working here, and in the 16th century there was a badger (a licensed corn dealer) and several joiners. Of the other craftsmen in Pulloxhill over the years, shoemakers and cordwainers, carpenters, blacksmiths and inevitably ale sellers were the most consistent and numerous. But by far the majority of the villagers worked on the land either as husbandmen and dairymen or as labourers.

⌘ RAVENSDEN

Most Bedfordshire villages are characterised by the many Ends, satellite hamlets centred around a central nucleus. Ravensden seems to have taken this characteristic to the extreme in that it is all Ends and no middle. Old hamlets are sprinkled around the boundary of the parish and the geographical centre of the parish is empty.

Most of the present population live in three distinct areas. Church End is the largest of these. The church is the oldest standing building, dating from before 1166, when Simon de Beauchamp, the Norman baron of Bedford Castle, included it among the 14 churches with which he endowed the newly founded Newnham Priory. It is in his foundation charter that Ravensden gets its earliest known mention in history and this probably marks the time when the scattered hamlets were drawn into the protection of one single parish.

The church's most interesting feature, architecturally, is probably the king-post roof structure, which is not common in this part of the country. What it does have is evidence of the work of local craftsmen, struggling over hard centuries to keep their church intact. Thus the timbers of the aforementioned king-post are rough hewn, the chancel arch is slightly off-centre with respect to the roof ridge, the simple tympanum over the south door has been reconstructed from two unmatching halves, one of which must have been salvaged from the now missing north door, and the walls are a patchwork of stones, tiles and bricks. The whole result is one of honest picturesqueness rather that stylised elegance, but the view, from the south, of Ravensden church on top of its hill, must be one of the most charming in the county. A Saxon brooch, now in Bedford Museum, was found in the garden of the vicarage here.

A few yards from the church stands the Horse and Jockey pub. This is now housed in a comfortable modern building, but it backs onto the thatched, timber-framed building, now a private house, which was its original home. There are not many of these old cottages left in Ravensden. Most of the population now live in the post-war villas which line both sides of the road from The Horse and Jockey to the northern end of the village at Northfields. Nevertheless, it is along this road that Ravensden's ghost is reported to walk – a figure seen from behind with her face concealed by a deep poke bonnet. When she turns towards the observer it is said that her face is indescribably horrible!

The commercial centre of Ravensden is the crossroads on the Kimbolton road, which was developed as a turnpike road at the beginning of the 19th century. Ravensden Crossroads must have started its life as the turnpike age equivalent of a motorway service station, with a blacksmith's shop to cater for horse and carriage and a public house to refresh the travellers.

The third populated area of Ravensden lies on the southern slope of Cleat Hill, along the Kimbolton road, just before it enters Bedford town. This group is saved from being absorbed into Bedford's suburban sprawl by Mowsbury Park and a little brook which marks the parish boundary. This brook is dominated on its northern side by a ridge known as Gray's Hill. The old road to Thurleigh runs along this ridge, past isolated farmhouses and cottages, to finish at Ravensden Wood-End. It is along this road that Ravensden's second ghost is said to walk, or rather ride, in a coach and four which drives from Wood-End to Thrayles End Farm, where the moat of the old manor house still exists.

⌘ RENHOLD

A long straggling village, greatly expanded, often referred to as 'righteous Renhold'. The village belonged to the Polhill estate and in 1919 the land was sold to tenant farmers and other villagers. There are still many thatched cottages, and a beautiful 17th century farmhouse at Salph End.

Salph End, Renhold

Where the Polhill Arms public house car park is today there was a brickworks and opposite the Three Horseshoes public house was a forge. The only other employment in Renhold used to be farm labouring for men, whilst the women went into service or found work in Bedford.

All Saints' church, whose first vicar was installed in 1220, stands proudly high among the trees at the east end of the village, surrounded by a neat, well-kept churchyard. It boasts a robed choir and a happy band of campanologists. Renhold chapel is at the far end of the village in Woodfield Lane. On special occasions the small congregation join for worship with members of the church.

⌘ RISELEY

It is apparent from records from the last century that Riseley was once almost completely self contained, having six general shops, two butchers, four bakers, one miller, one nurse, one doctor, one surgeon and one dentist. As well as the parish church there were originally three other chapels, Moravian, Wesleyan (now Methodist) and Baptist. At the latter those offering themselves for baptism, sat in a chair fitted on the end of a long pole for total immersion!

There was a working windmill on Keysoe Hill, operated by the brothers Ken and Fred Rootham. This was an old design which involved the use of much muscle power to release a large lever allowing the sails to turn into the wind.

'Riseley Feast' was held on the last Sunday in July; it included setting up a fun fair on the green that weekend, and the custom continued until the outbreak of the First World War. The village population numbered some 500 at this period, but was depleted when the men were called up, leaving only two on each farm. Twenty-two men did not return from the war – mostly youngsters.

In 1942 five American bases were set up on airfields in the immediate vicinity, with about 3,000 men at each. On 14th October 1943 one of the returning American B17 aircraft actually crash-landed in the village.

The village is not unique in having its own charity, but perhaps the charity itself is. It started as a bequest by Thomas Bourne of Riseley, who during the early 1800s invested a sum of money in $2^1/_2$% Consuls, bequeathing in his will the interest to the 'widows or Riseley' for ever. Before decimalisation this amounted to 5s 4d per year amongst 30 widows. The trustee appointed by the Parish Council no doubt augmented the income sufficiently for them to receive threepence each! With the coming of decimal currency there were 36 widows who received 1p each. This state of affairs continued until the 'Widows Mite' charity as it is called amalgamated with a Riseley church charity to distribute a more realistic sum. The original church-sponsored 'Bread for the Poor' charity now takes the form of hot cross buns distributed on Good Friday to all those attending church.

Since the end of the Second World War, Riseley, like many other Bedfordshire villages, has grown a little, with several small estates appearing. The population increase is mainly due to improved facilities, particularly transport. The nature of farming has changed to nearly entirely arable, with many large hedgeless fields of oil seed rape and wheat being grown. A few farms still keep sheep, while only a very small number keep cattle or pigs.

Gradually the rural appearance of the High Street has changed with the arrival of a tarmac road surface, electricity cables on overhead poles, mains water, main sewer and street lighting.

⌘ ROXTON

Rich in history, this village in the Ouse Valley progressed enormously last century. As a Saxon settlement it suffered from the raiding Danes who proceeded up river from the Wash. The inhabitants moved westwards and tilled the fertile soil that still grows high quality vegetables and grain. In the last century little girls as young as eight years became very skilled at pillow lace making, learning the craft from their mothers. All the men worked on the land; it was their whole way of life.

The 20th century slowly brought a change of prospects, Roxton being one of the first districts to grow Brussels sprouts, that popular winter vegetable. The Delap family owned the village farms and cottages, but in the early 1920s the estate was

Roxton's thatched chapel

nearly all sold to the various tenants. Twenty market gardeners grew vegetables for the London and northern markets, in the summer horses and carts going via Ford Lane over the river at Tempsford Anchor en route to Tempsford Great Northern station. It became almost a ritual to attend St Neots' market on Thursdays and Bedford on Saturdays. Alas you will no longer see cattle grazing in river meadows, and the only horses to be seen are riding horses. In 1907 some 40 horses were kept at Park Farm, but the faithful old carthorse has given way to the latest tractor, and the gleaning bell rung from the parish church tower at sunrise and sunset is a memory of the past.

After the Second World War thoughts were directed to the building of a parish hall for social activities. Men of the village, by voluntary labour, built a good functional hall; run by trustees representing every organisation, it is still a huge success. Sixteen old-type houses beyond renovation were demolished and new council houses built for families, and bungalows and flats provided for the elderly.

Cricket is considered of the highest importance in the village and has been for well over a hundred years, the team being allowed to play in Roxton Park, a wonderful sight on a summer's afternoon, an oasis of grass and trees.

⌘ SHARNBROOK

Sharnbrook is a large village in the north of the county, just off the main A6 road, with the river Ouse flowing to the south.

There has been a settlement here since at least Saxon times. In the 12th century the Knights Templars held land here, followed by the Knights Hospitallers until the Reformation. In the 17th century mat making was a local craft, using rushes from the river banks.

High Street grandeur at Sharnbrook

The parish church of St Peter is Norman, enlarged in the 13th century. It had a more impressive tower built in the 14th century and the church itself was restored in 1855. It has a large north chapel and outside in the churchyard can be found the Magniac family mausoleum. The Magniacs owned Colworth Manor House in the 19th century.

In the course of its history every village has produced its 'characters' and Sharnbrook is no exception. Such a one was Katie Partridge, still very much alive in the memory of the older people of Sharnbrook. Katie lived in a drab little cottage opening onto the west side of the High Street, a splendid vantage point for keeping an eye on village comings and goings.

Katie on her bicycle was one of the sights of the village. Perched on its rickety frame she was a menace to all road users. The middle of the road was hers and any following motorists had to guess which way she was turning.

Frank Mole, the celebrated watercolour artist, always stayed with Katie when he came to Sharnbrook to paint. Perhaps he enjoyed her talk as well as her cooking.

She was a staunch supporter of the church and could be found every Sunday morning sitting bolt upright in the front pew, doubtless criticising the singing and the sermon. She died in August 1969 and is buried beside her mother in the churchyard near the Marriott Memorial Gate. Katie's cottage has gone as well, with its neighbour, the Half Moon pub, both now converted into Half Moon Cottage. Mention her name in the village even today and someone is sure to laugh and say, 'Oh, Katie Patridge, she was a character!' – and so she was.

⌘ SHEFFORD

Sheep-ford is now known as Shefford, and is a busy market community with the friendliness of a village that now enjoys the benefit of a bypass. Its origin stems from various sheep crossings and the shepherds' tracks took on the appearance of primitive roads, eventually creating a trading centre. The right to hold a market was granted in the 13th century and every Friday morning stallholders arrive early to erect their stalls, hoping the weather will be fair enough to lure people out to be tempted by the carefully displayed goods. Shefford is flat country and the wind can whistle down the High Street at what seems like hurricane force on occasions.

Once the town was enclosed by three bridges – two of which still exist over the rivers Hitt and Flitt, while the other was a railway bridge which spanned the High Street and carried passengers and freight from Hitchin to Bedford. The bridge became redundant after the closure of the railway and was dismantled. There was a certain irony in this, as the coming of the railway had effectively killed off the extensive use of the canal and the barges which carried coal to the area from Kings Lynn.

There are three main wide streets and these still possess a number of good red-brick buildings. Among these are public houses which are relics from the days when Shefford was a busy post town on the thoroughfare to Bedford, where the London–Northampton coaches stopped by to refresh their passengers. A newcomer will be

The Porch, Shefford

told about all the inns there were but the number will vary from 14 to 40. One of the old pubs is now the bank – a 16th century arcaded brick and timber building. It is picturesque and difficult to recognise as a bank and only the familiar lettering identifies it as one of the country's leading financial establishments.

There are not many sheep in evidence around Shefford nowadays, the surrounding area being mainly arable. The countryside is open, and spring and early summer see the glowing, waving fields of various crops basking in the sunshine. There are pockets of woods where walkers can follow a nature trail or exercise their dogs, and picnic areas where families can spend a few happy hours.

Shefford has a very colourful history, and numerous locally well-known figures, but the only nationally known person was the poet Robert Bloomfield, famous for his poem *The Farmer's Boy*, who lived in Shefford for about 20 years. He died in 1823 and is buried in Campton churchyard, since it was only in 1903 that Shefford was considered to be a separate parish and in fact until that time had been regarded as the 'poor relation' to Campton.

⌘ SHILLINGTON

Mention Shillington to most people and they will say, 'Ah yes, the church on the hill.' It dominates the view from any approach into the village. The hill on which All Saints' church stands was of considerable strategic importance in earlier times, with Roman pottery and early British coins having been found in the early 19th century. The origins of the church itself are somewhat obscure, though research suggests that initially a pagan temple existed next to the watch tower and that there was a Christian church on the hill at a very early date.

Regarding the foundation of the church, legend has it that originally the plan was to build it at Church Pannell (an ancient earthwork between Shillington and Gravenhurst) but each night the Devil moved the stone up the hill until the builders finally succumbed and built it in its present location. What is certain is that apart from the north wall and tower the church that was finally built in the 1400s is the one that stands today.

Shillington was a close knit agricultural community with most farms being tenanted. Poverty was common but the church remained the focal point of village life. In Norman times Shillington consisted of tiny hamlets all within the same boundary but each one is as individual in character as the next. Two miles south of Shillington lies the group of houses called Pegsden whilst Stondon and Holwell were part of the village for centuries.

Being in an agricultural community, most of the men worked on the farms in a variety of jobs: horse keeping, ploughing, stack building and harvesting. Those not working on the farms were employed in the building of Welwyn Garden City, which meant a long cycle journey morning and night. A few adventurous young men upped and travelled to Jersey in the spring to dig potatoes! Services to the village were very good then and included 4 bakers, 3 butchers, 2 blacksmiths, a wheelwright, an undertaker, a saddler, 2 shoemakers, 6 general stores, 8 public houses and of course 3 chapels and the church. What a contrast to today with more houses, and more people but greatly reduced services.

⌘ SILSOE

The name of the village is from Old English *hoh* 'hill-spur' and the personal name Sifel, i.e. Sifel's hill-spur. The Danes were thought to have been among the earliest settlers here. The village's later history, however, is very much bound up with that of the de Grey family who owned the Wrest estate, an association which was to span six centuries.

The village's growth was largely influenced by the needs of the Wrest estate, and most of the inhabitants were servants, gardeners, stable hands and blacksmiths who lived in thatched, terraced cottages, some of which exist today.

By the mid 19th century a number of trades were being plied in the village. The suitability of the soil made market gardening an important occupation. There was a baker, very well known locally, who supplied Wrest House, and people travelled from many surrounding villages to buy his excellent bread. In the roof of the old

Wrest House, Silsoe

bakehouse, now a private dwelling, the ventilator can still be seen. There was also a butcher who bought in and slaughtered animals, and his slaughterhouse is still in existence. The village's and estate's other needs were served by a milkman, cobbler, draper, builder, grocer and blacksmith. The estate, in its turn, provided the village with a church, a school and a row of almshouses, so sited that the cottages were hidden from the gentry's view as they drove to church in nearby Flitton.

A change in the fortunes of the village came about with the death in the First World War of Lord Lucas, the last male member of the de Grey dynasty. During the war, Wrest House was used as a military hospital, but afterwards Lady Lucas was obliged to sell the house and estate. During the ensuing years it fell into disrepair but is now restored. The park and some of the state rooms are open to the public during summer weekends. The present open fields surrounding the park replace the heavily wooded land which was cleared as part of the 'war effort'.

The present Wrest House, situated in a splendid park landscaped by Lancelot 'Capability' Brown, has superseded two others, the first being recorded in the Domesday Book in 1086. In 1319 a royal charter was granted for a weekly market to be held there and a twice-yearly fair, to which came traders from Bedford and Luton.

Silsoe church stands on the site of a much earlier 12th to 13th century building which had a central tower. In the early 19th century Earl de Grey wished to embellish it with a spire but the weight of the structure proved too much for the walls and the whole building collapsed. The church was rebuilt and completed in 1830. Most of its stained glass windows represent the families of Wrest House.

Silsoe is known worldwide as the centre of agricultural engineering in Britain. The National Institute of Agricultural Engineering arrived 1947 and was followed in 1964 by the National College of Agricultural Engineering. It is now a faculty of Cranfield University, with a main emphasis on postgraduate studies.

The village can even boast a 'cage', built in 1795 as a temporary lock-up for stray animals and drunks, and to its central pole were chained prisoners in transit between Bedford and Luton.

No village would be complete without its ghost and Silsoe is host to at least two. A beautiful grey lady walks the present George Hotel, once a house attached to Wrest Park, and, in Silsoe House nearby, the ghost of a small fair haired girl has been seen several times looking for her adored nurse who was dismissed and for whom the child pined and died.

⌘ SOUTHILL

Southill is an interesting village, bounded on the south by the river Flitt and on the east by the Ivel.

Southill House was once the home of the Byng family, whose most famous, or infamous, member was Admiral John Byng, executed on board his own ship in

Southill House – elegance by Henry Holland

1757. In the 1790s the Whitbread family came to Southill and the house was remodelled for them, till it was what Pevsner calls 'one of the most exquisite English understatements'. The work was done by Henry Holland and the grounds were landscaped by Capability Brown. Southill House is now the private residence of the Whitbread family and neither the house nor the park are open the public.

In the village itself was the church of All Saints, estate cottages and the Southill poorhouse or workhouse. In 1801 there was a terrible harvest failure and bread became very expensive, so that magistrates in the northern division of Bedfordshire recommended that parishes give their paupers a meal of meat, potato and rice – for a family of five or six this meant $1\frac{1}{2}$lb of meat, 2lb of potato and a $\frac{1}{4}$lb of rice between them for one meal.

One common complaint against workhouses was that they gave labourers a better meal than they could possibly afford if they had a job and provided for themselves. In some cases this was true, as many labourers could only afford a tiny piece of meat once a week, that usually being fatty bacon, to supplement their meagre diet of bread and potatoes.

⌘ STEVINGTON

Stevington is an attractive stone-built village bordered to the north by the river Ouse and lying about five miles north-west of Bedford. The visitor approaching from Bedford will notice on the left the windmill. It is a post mill (revolves on a central post) and was in operation until about 1936. Bedfordshire County Council acquired the mill in 1951 and restored it, but had to fit a lightning conductor as a safety precaution and this is the only thing that prevents the mill revolving and being in full working order today.

Work found in the tower of St Mary's parish church confirms that there was a settlement here in Saxon times. It is a lovely church and among the interesting items are the early 16th century carved wooden bench ends of men and animals preserved from the old pews. There is a holy well set in a recess in the boundary wall of the churchyard and it was a place of pilgrimage in the Middle Ages. The water was sought for its healing powers for eye afflictions. The spring, which still feeds the well, has never been known to freeze or run dry.

In the centre of the village there is an old stone cross, which gives rise to the village nickname – Spike Island. It is thought to be the cross which Christian in *The Pilgrim's Progress* 'came to and loosened his burden from off his shoulders'. It is the focal point for the village.

Well into the 20th century the village had a bakehouse, working mill, blacksmith, wheelwright, carpenters and women who made and sold pillow lace. There were door-to-door vendors of groceries, haberdashery, ironmongery and the Hat Man from Luton called in spring and autumn and carried his hats in large cardboard boxes. Activities marked the passing months of the year; Plough Monday, the Crowning of the May Queen, Sunday school treats and the Camp meeting – an open air service given by the Methodist circuit.

Walking along the starlit roads at night one can easily believe in the local ghost stories. There is a 'Sandeman Port' type figure who flits among the shadows and in a house near the cross a miserly old man lived who hoarded his cash. He suddenly became ill and was rushed to hospital. He died there and it is thought his ghost sometimes returns to his home to look for his money.

There is a railway line which ran from Bedford to Northampton just south of the village and this has now been turned into a country walk much used by the locals. Being on high ground it affords excellent views of the surrounding countryside.

⌘ STEWARTBY

Prior to the year 1935 the village of Stewartby was known as Wootton Pillinge, and up to about 1926 it was no more than a small hamlet comprising two or three farms and a dozen or more cottages. Eight of these cottages were known as Forders Villas (since demolished) and were for key workers of the then Pillenge Brickworks owned by Messrs Forders. Members of the Stewart family were amongst the principal directors.

Concern about the wellbeing of the labour force led the Stewart family to embark on the building of a Model Village which we now know as Stewarby. The first 50 or so dwellings were built in 1926 to a very high standard for the time, all having large gardens, flush toilets and bathrooms. The dwellings were spacious and open plan and were for renting at low cost to brickworks personnel only. They were located close to the brickworks. The village Memorial Hall was built in

Stewartby

1929 and was paid for by the Brick Company and maintained by them with a resident caretaker.

During the year 1934 HRH Prince George visited the brickworks and at the same time opened the village fountain (no longer working) in the closed area now known as Churchill Close. The development of the Model Village now accelerated and in 1935 'Stewartby' was born, being formed by taking in all of Wootton Pillinge and parts of Wootton and Kempston.

Further development of the village took place up to the outbreak of the Second World War. The village now comprised some 210 dwellings, all built to high specifications, all owned by the Brick Company and rented to employees only. The village boasted a very smart hall, two schools, doctors' surgery, resident nurse and policeman, swimming pool, sports club, post office and general store.

No further development of the village took place during the war years. Shortly after the war ended all the existing closes in the village were named after the national war leaders. The main road through the village was named Stewartby Way.

The year 1951 saw the building and dedication of Stewartby United Church. Prior to this religious services had been held in the village hall and a small chapel on the outskirts of the village. In 1951–2 a major building programme was again undertaken by the Brick Company. This consisted of a new estate comprising 70 houses – together with the laying of new roads – again all for renting to employees of the Brick Company at low cost. This was the last major house building programme undertaken by the Brick Company.

At about 1955–6 the Sir Malcolm Stewart Trust was created and as a result the building of a number of bungalows was commenced, designed by the distinguished architect Sir Albert Richardson.

In the late 1960s a worked-out quarry which had filled with water was leased to the local authority and Stewartby Water Sports Association was formed. This is now a thriving club and the area has been landscaped to form a Country Park.

Due to changes of policy within the Brick Company and the now natural desire for families to own their own properties, the decision was made to sell off their entire stock of rented dwellings, existing tenants being offered favourable purchase terms. A third of the tenants availed themselves of this opportunity and the remaining property is now on the open market.

Stewartby is built on an open plan system with large green areas and like the rest of Bedfordshire claims a John Bunyan connection, which in this case is a pond where he is supposed to have washed his feet.

⌘ STOPSLEY

Stopsley today is a thriving community on the north-eastern outskirts of Luton. Travelling through its centre on the fast dual carriageway of the A505 between Hitchin and Dunstable, an observer can see little in Stopsley's modern offices and shops of the generations who have survived the hard rural life, plague, famine and war since the Stone Age.

These early settlers, whose remains and artefacts have been discovered in the Mixies Hill area, would have found a chalk ridge covered with oak forest and dotted with gorse, a healthier spot than the damp Lea valley below, where Luton was to grow. It must have needed hard long work with rudimentary tools to clear the area sufficiently to allow the heavy clay soil littered with flints to be farmed.

Over the centuries, the land cleared by many became held by a handful of families, two of whom, the Crawleys and the de Somerys, gave their names to locations in the area. In Stoppelee in the Hundred of Flitt, cattle and crops of wheat, barley, oats and beans each played their part in the agricultural round, but it was the high quality of the straw from the Upper Chalklands which was to determine the course of Stopsley's and, of course, Luton's development in the 19th century.

In the early years of Victoria's reign, London manufacturers went to the Far East for cheap straw plait, but these markets collapsed in the second half of the century, forcing the London firms to look closer to home for supplies. Whilst the Stopsley men worked on the land, or at the local brickworks, producing by hand the plum-coloured 'Luton Greys' so typical in the town, their wives put aside their lace making and turned to the more lucrative straw plait. By the century's turn, the original foreign markets were again exporting but hat firms had sprung up in Luton and the industry here had acquired an impetus of its own. Children were taught to plait straw at school and had to complete their share before going out to play. Their mothers would pass the plait through the mills, machines like small wooden mangles, to soften it for hat making.

What little spare time the villagers had was spent in the main at the three churches: St Thomas', the Baptist church and the Methodist chapel, at the three pubs: the Brickmakers, the Sportsman and the First and Last, or on their vegetable patches, some complete with pig and poultry. There were weekly whist drives, magic lantern shows, football and cricket matches in their season, but it was the annual festivals such as May Day which really brought the villagers together.

But times were changing. By the onset of the Second World War, Stopsley was looking increasingly towards Luton for work and leisure. The old festivals were no longer celebrated. Powdrill's brickworks in St Thomas' Road was soon to close down. Houses had been built on the fields which had hitherto separated the two communities. By 1945, farming had become fully mechanised and the post-war years were to see a decline in the hat trade. But Luton had established itself as an industrial and commercial centre in other fields, especially through Vauxhall Motors.

The urbanisation of Stopsley was formally recognised in 1933 when the village became incorporated into Luton. Yet although the pond and green have disappeared under a roundabout and virtually all the houses are post-1903, Stopsley has retained its own identity, distinct from Luton. And the countryside is still here, only a few minutes' walk from the village centre.

⌘ STREATLEY

To the outside world Streatley as a village did not exist until the latter half of the 19th century. Until then the area known as Streatley ('clearing by the Roman road') was no more than a scattered farming hamlet, consisting of a few dwellings tucked away in a fold of the downs set back from the edge of the Chiltern hills.

The oldest building is St Margaret's church, its northern and southern doorways, and east and west aisle windows dating from the 14th century. The nave windows, however, date from the 15th century, as does the tower, also the roofs of the nave and aisles. The font is mid-13th century and presumably comes from an earlier church on the site.

Probably due to the Enclosure Acts, plague and agricultural depressions, the church fell into ruins at least twice. The major work of restoration was done in 1938 under the direction of Sir Albert Richardson as a memorial to Arthur Parnell, who, as Archdeacon of Bedford, was responsible for restoring many of Bedfordshire's churches.

The village school, built in 1882 on the edge of the village to accommodate children from both Streatley and the nearby village of Sharpenhoe, was demolished in 1986. Three houses now take up the space that was once school and playground.

People remember when after-school activities in the summer amounted to a game of 'Hare and Hounds', a form of paperchase. This was enjoyed by almost the entire school across the surrounding hills and fields. A cricket match, married men against the single, would provide bank holiday entertainment, with a prize of 10s provided by Tommy McIntosh if a ball could be knocked clean over his barns alongside the field where the game was played at Sharpenhoe. In winter a football

Looking towards Streatley and the Chiltern Hills

match with the boys from Barton would be played in whichever field was down to grass and invariably resulted in a win for Barton.

With the church in ruins, the only place for worship was the small Baptist chapel, or, alternatively, services were held in a green wooden hut in front of and belonging to the Chequers public house.

Behind the granary barns that stood where Stanley Road now is, Mr Swain kept his store of coal with which he supplied the village. The village boasted a blacksmith, Mr Kingham, who eked out a precarious living in his forge almost opposite Stanley Road. A group of children would always be found standing around the open doors, fascinated by the smells and sparks coming from within the dark interior, decorated by long forgotten show certificates and shoes for the horses that formed his regular customers.

Recorded in the vestry book is a fine for digging a saw-pit on the village green, opposite to which was a great walnut tree, a delight to the younger generation in the autumn. To the left of the green, close by the wall of Streatley House, stood the village pump, the source of drinking water for the village unless you had your own well. The pump was supplied from the spring, whose waters still surface, laying icy patches for the unwary.

In pre-war days the village boundaries stretched from Barton to Luton and tremendous expansion took place at that time. Within the village itself there were probably three times as many houses by 1939 than in 1900. With the Second World

War came many changes. Evacuees arrived in force and many of the empty houses at Warden Hill were commandeered for their use. Probably the most significant event for the future development of the community spirit of the village was the formation of the youth club, which after the war developed into the village hall.

With the war over, further development took place within the village and once again it almost doubled in size. It is now an attractive, largely unspoilt village in an area of outstanding natural beauty.

⌘ SUNDON

Sundon is in the south of the county, in the area of Chiltern chalk, and it is necessary to climb considerably to get to the village, which is about 500 feet above sea level.

At least four blacksmiths have given their services from the forge in Streatley Road. As well as shoeing the horses the blacksmith would repair the farm machinery and make little iron fences to border the graves in the churchyard. On a happier note he would make iron hoops for the boys to bowl along and smaller wooden ones for the girls. One of the fourpenny iron hoops has survived to this day.

When the primary school opened in 1874, the master had a difficult beginning to overcome. The boys did weeding and the girls went straw plaiting in a little cottage near the Baptist chapel in Streatey Road. Towards the end of the last century three little girls were burnt to death when an ember fell from the fire while they were asleep, worn out from straw plaiting. Miss Prudden used to sit in her cottage in Slate Hall doing her plaiting. A tall tree on the edge of the Paddock in Common Lane was regularly used for the correct measuring of the plait before the plait was taken by the carrier to Luton Plait Market.

Lord Sundon, Clerk to the Treasury, and Lady Sundon, 'Woman of the Bedchamber' to Queen Caroline of Anspach and a personal friend of the Duchess of Marlborough, entertained many famous people at their mansion in Lower Sundon. Lord Sundon's account books have been preserved and they shed a great light upon Georgian affairs, revealing such items as wine purchased by the hogshead and a periwig bought for his father's birthday. He paid for the mansion in instalments and often paid the mason for work on his house. When the Duke of Marlborough died, a £500 legacy was accepted by Lord Sundon. After his death, his niece, Elizabeth Cole, inherited a quarter share of the manor. She lived there for a time with her husband William and it was during this time that John Wesley, the famous preacher visited them often. William and John were at Charterhouse School together.

Sundon has always been blessed with real characters able to laugh at themselves and to make other people laugh. Much of this mirth took place in the local pubs. Mrs Smith was landlady at the old Crown. She opened on Sundays but would not serve anyone that had used the Red Lion or White Hart during the week!

⌘ SUTTON

Though Sutton is a small village, just one street, it has a great deal of historic interest. It was given, along with neighbouring Potton, to the Burgoyne family by John o' Gaunt himself and Burgoynes lived in Sutton Park (now the John o' Gaunt Golf Course) until the family died out just before the Second World War. One, Sir John Burgoyne, became famous for his rescue of the Empress Eugenie (wife of Napoleon III) in 1870. General Sir John Burgoyne was not so lucky. He lost to the Americans in the Battle of Saratoga during the American War of Independence.

All Saints' church is the proud possessor of a sacred barrel organ (dated 1820). It is in perfect working order and could well be used for services, provided there was someone with enough stamina to pump and turn the handle through umpteen verses of each hymn!

Between the Old Rectory and the playing field there is a narrow strip of land known as the Bull Run or Bull Yard. It was presumably the place where the village bull was kept. True to stockmarket tradition of bulls and bears being opposite, the village Bear Pit was right at the far end of the village from the Bull Run. There is no sign of the bear pit now, though it is shown on some old maps. Apparently the bears were brought into the pit through a tunnel under the road. Now, all the that remains to show the place is a row of cottages known as The Bear Gardens.

Sutton's medieval packhorse bridge and the ford

The Bull Run and the Bear Pit are separated by Sutton's most famous landmark – the medieval packhorse bridge and ford. These attract many visitors in the warm weather, especially those with children.

The ford is less popular with the locals when, after spells of heavy rain, they drive to the brink only to find that the water level has risen dramatically and they have to make a $2^1/_2$ mile detour!

As one might expect in so historic a place, there is a resident ghost (not that he appears very often). He is supposed to be the ghost of one of two Cavaliers who were trying to escape the Roundheads by leaving the Old Manor House via an underground passage leading from the manor to the church and possibly beyond. Unfortunately for them the Roundheads must have known about the passage, for when the Cavaliers emerged they were promptly killed. The existence of the passage seems reasonably certain. When a large, long, deep hole appeared in Sutton Park (big enough to take a cow) it was believed to be caused by the caving in of the passage roof. Then, during the incumbency of the Rev. Claude Davis, what appeared to be part of the tunnel was discovered during repairs to the church floor. Unfortunately it was deemed too dangerous to explore and was duly sealed up.

One Sutton character who (alas) was only too human was the 'Wicked Rector', Edward Drax Free, incumbent here from 1808 to 1830. He was sued by the churchwardens for lewdness, indecency, fighting in the church, keeping pigs in the churchyard, keeping fodder in the church porch, keeping pigeons in the belfry and selling lead from the church roof. As Edward was also a lawyer he usually won his cases! It came to such a state of affairs that Edward became virtually a prisoner in the rectory, with armed churchwardens patrolling the grounds. He can not have been unpopular with everyone though because he was kept fed and watered (so the story goes) by the village children, who sneaked into the rectory garden while the churchwardens' backs were turned, and put food and drink into a basket which Edward let down on the end of a rope from an upstairs window.

⌘ TEMPSFORD

Tempsford can boast more than a thousand years of history. Here the Roman road passes through the village. When the Romans went, the Danes came. One of the most formidable fortifications of these Viking conquerors was constructed at Tempsford. But in the mid-10th century, five centuries after the Romans had gone as an occupying power, it was precisely here that a Danish chieftain was defeated.

There has been a house on the site of Tempsford Hall for only 200 years or so, for the old manor house in the village used to stand down by the river, near Tempsford Lock. There is a thumbnail sketch of this house on the map of Bedfordshire engraved by William Gordon in 1736, and the old house seems to have been a three-storeyed Jacobean building, with wings at either end, and a central tunnel.

However, all was changed when Sir Gillies Payne brought the estate in 1769 with part of the family fortune gained from sugar and slaves in the West Indies. In 1794 when Sir Gillies made his will, he mentioned his new-built mansion house in Tempsford as well as the old house near the river.

The Hall was extensively rebuilt in 1874, but all was burnt down in a devastating fire in 1898. It was completely gutted and took over three years to rebuild. It was erected on the same ground but redesigned and built in mellow red brickwork with a tiled roof and stone mullioned windows. The interior contained beautiful oak carved panels, many of which can still be seen today.

In 1940 Tempsford saw the rebirth of 138 Squadron. This was the first of the Moon Squadrons, set up on 20th August, in answer to Winston Churchill's famous directive: 'Set Europe ablaze!' Brave men and women set out from Tempsford to parachute into Europe. Last minute preparation – issue of French clothes, parachute, forged papers, even lethal pills – was carried out in specially reconstructed outbuildings at Gibraltar Farm, on the eastern boundary of the airfield. It was a remarkable fact that Tempsford, one of the most secret airfields in Britain during the Second World War, was never, according to station records, attacked by enemy aircraft. This was not because it was hidden from view to the outsider. Every day hundreds of passengers had a grandstand view of its activities from trains running on the main LNER line to Scotland. It seems hard to believe that no enemy agents ever reported its existence. The nearest enemy action was a V1 flying bomb that flew over on 16th October 1944 before crashing near St Neots.

Accommodation and briefing was given under the utmost secrecy at Tempsford Hall. A memorial plaque can be seen in the only remaining barn at Gilbraltar Farm and there is another plaque in St Peter's church.

⌘ THURLEIGH

Sometime long ago, when much of England was covered in forest and scrub, men came to where a gentle slope rose from a winding river for about three miles to the north-east, onto a plateau. Here they cleared the trees to allow a good range of vision over the surrounding land and called this place 'the clearing in the wood'.

The Romans came and left traces in the area that is now Vicarage Green and later a church began to rise to the glory of God and also as look-out and shelter against potential enemies. What a task! Stone must have been hauled from at least seven miles away.

Perhaps because this plateau had such a wide outlook, it was chosen as an ideal spot for a castle stronghold. Not much is recorded of this castle and its activities, but it must have acted as a fortress to protect its citizens. The castle mound, probably of stone and earth, was built behind the church to raise it even higher

High Street, Thurleigh

above the surrounding countryside and a protective moat was dug all round. Although by now its size and height is considerably reduced, the mound is still there, called Bury Hill.

And so Thurleigh remained small and insignificant over the centuries as men continued to dwell here and farm the heavy soil. Then with the Second World War came an airfield, with its large hangars and sprawl of prefabricated huts, and in 1942 the Americans arrived.

Many stories evolved round the activities, told and retold, including the tale of the burning corn. Planes carrying wounded could have priority landing if a flare was dropped as they circled to land. One such flare accidentally fell into a field of stooked corn and set it alight. A plough and tractor stood in the field ready for use, so the quick-thinking farmer's son promptly drew a ring of ploughing around the fire. Another tells of tragedy when two planes collided in mid-air with full loads, killing all their crew. There were individual heroes too, for Sergeant 'Snuffy' Smith won the first Congressional Medal of Honour awarded in the European conflict in a mission from Thurleigh. He is buried in Arlington Cemetery, the resting place of President Kennedy.

Thurleigh is still playing a part in our country's defence for much of the plateau is now used by the Royal Aircraft Establishment.

⌘ TINGRITH

Tingrith is one of the smallest villages in Bedfordshire though the changes since the

Old School House, Tingrith

1960s have been very noticeable. This is now a conservation area and all electricity and telephone services have gone underground. However, there is one thing that will probably not alter and that is the old red telephone box, now subject to a preservation order. The lovely 12th century church, with its beautiful stained glass, oak beams and polished brass, is, of course, unchanging too.

Shopping habits have become very different over the years. At one time there were literally visits from the butcher, the baker, the candlestick maker and there was also a village shop and post office. Now nearly everybody goes to the nearest superstore in Flitwick.

The pace of life in Tingrith has become quicker over the years, but it is still very rural. There is nothing nicer on a spring or summer evening than to come here after a busy day and relax, while the only sounds you can hear are the birds singing and the breeze in the trees.

⌘ TODDINGTON

Ask anyone who has driven through Toddington what is his lasting impression, and it will have to be the large village green, guarded by the parish church. The basic

85

Toddington Manor

form of the green has remained unchanged for hundreds of years. Local people still refer to one of the crossings as 'the gravel path'. Now in a conservation area, many of the buildings remain almost unchanged, but many more have disappeared; gone are the fire station, the kitchen, the pound and several cottages which surrounded the pond.

The town hall has suffered many changes, the bell tower having been removed when it was re-roofed in the early 1960s. Before it became unsafe for use in the late 1960s, the large upstairs room was used for public functions. It has now been sympathetically restored and forms a private enclave in the middle of parish land.

On the green, the village pump still stands. Nearby is the former forge – behind which was sited the pound. Fairs were held on the green in past years, as well as the weekly market. Now the green is booked nearly every Saturday in the summer by various village organisations for market stalls. These stalls are usually sited in front of 'Diggles' seat. Before retiring, Diggles was mostly connected with agriculture and he became the unofficial village molecatcher. After retiring, Diggles could always be found sitting on the same seat on the green, accompanied by his dog, with a cheery word for all who passed by. Diggles belonged to a time when nearly every local had a nickname, and when most men were employed at the local cement works. This works formed the main alternative employment for men, other than agriculture, until the coming of the motor trade to Luton.

Toddington's most famous historical character was Lady Henrietta Wentworth. She became the mistress of the Duke of Monmouth, who often visited her at Toddington Manor. There still stands what is reputed to be the Monmouth Oak, where legend says he carved her initials. Henrietta lived openly with him in France. The Duke was the eldest natural son of King Charles II. Following the Battle of Sedgemoor and the subsequent execution of the Duke, Lady Henrietta returned to Toddington Manor and died of a broken heart shortly afterwards. The whole affair scandalised many – the bell ropes were cut so that the bells could not be rung for her funeral. Her tomb is in the Wentworth Chapel and the words on it emphasise that she died unmarried.

A curiosity in Toddington's churchyard is the tombstone to Joyce Foll, which states that she died on *31st April* 1853.

From the green a lane leads to Conger Hill, which is the remains of a motte and bailey castle. For generations children from the village schools have climbed the hill at noon on Shrove Tuesday to listen to the witch frying her pancakes. So too on this day the shriving bell was tolled.

There are many records of the straw plait industry in the village. In early days there was a plait room in the workhouse, employing the poor. Later a plait school was formed in the small St George's hall near the church, where children received some measure of education. Residents were involved in Luton's hat industry and Toddington also had its families of thatchers and other rural occupations.

There have been many changes over the years, but in spite of the extensive housing developments, Toddington still retains its very special village atmosphere around the ancient green.

⌘ TOTTERNHOE

Totternhoe is a straggling village that has three ends – Church End, Middle End and Lower End! The main road through the village lies along the foot of the hills which carry on westward from Dunstable Downs and end abruptly at Totternhoe Knolls. Standing up there on the Knolls, at the highest point, with the ground dropping sharply away on three sides, it is easy to see why the Saxons used it as a look-out point, which gave the village its name, and why the Normans built Bedfordshire's strongest castle on this spot. But the fortifications were of timber and the Normans never replaced them with stone buildings as they did in many other places, so that now all that remains is the mound on which the wooden keep once stood, surrounded by a moat, and the outline of the outer and inner baileys and the garth, or field, where the animals grazed.

Below the castle mound, on the other side of the road, the ground slopes gently down to the Meads and the stream, once called the riddy, one of those which runs into the river Ouzel. Over to the left is the cluster of houses along the road leading to the church of St Giles, with its tower just visible through the trees. And still further over is the tower of the mill which lost its sails in a gale in 1880. But beyond these is a magnificent view of the Vale of Aylesbury to the west, across to Leighton Buzzard to the north and towards the A5 and the hills beyond on the east. Just below the hill on this side are the kilns of the lime works which now quarry chalk near the site where the old stone quarries worked for centuries. In the Middle Ages Totternhoe stone was used in many a church in Bedfordshire and Hertfordshire, as well as St Albans Abbey and even the 'King's houses' in Windsor.

Like most villages Totternhoe is a mixture of old and new. There are no very large houses – even the house once known as the Chief Mansion House is not as big as you might expect from its rather grand title – but there are some attractive cottages and farmhouses, or houses which once belonged to farms. They are mostly brick and timber buildings, originally with thatched roofs, though many of them have by now had their thatch replaced by tiles and their bricks painted white. Most of the building though is post-war, for the village has grown tremendously since 1950.

Until the Second World War the village was a mass of orchards – plum trees were grown everywhere and many cottages paid their rent with the proceeds of the plum crop. One old lady remembers coming to Totternhoe as a child for the first time when the blossom was out and thinking it looked like fairyland. The plums were sold to hat manufacturers for dyeing. They certainly make delicious jam, but now there are only old trees left in gardens and fields and the fruit is often left to rot where it falls.

But it is the Knolls for which many older people who grew up in this part of Bedfordshire remember Totternhoe, and all the Sunday School outings and excursions that used to go there. From Luton, Dunstable and Leighton Buzzard and all around they flocked to Totternhoe Knolls. When the village was enclosed in 1892, the hill where the Normans had built their castle was kept as an area for public recreation and it became a favourite spot for picnics and walks and outings.

Now the area is a nature reserve and on a weekday the occasional walker out with the dog, or the rider on his horse, are the only visitors. There are more at weekends, of course, and sometimes a local rambling club walks this way. The Sunday School outings come no more, but the orchids and butterflies and all the other flora and fauna unique to the chalk downland are the delight of the naturalists and conservationists.

⌘ TURVEY

Turvey is a pleasant riverside village on the borders of Bedfordshire and Buckinghamshire. Set in undulating countryside, the houses and cottages built in limestone have steep, red tiled roofs and wide eaves. The village is surrounded by parkland with many fine specimen trees. The meaning of the name Turvey is thought to be 'land of good turf at the bend of a river'. An early crossing by a

The Three Fyshes, Turvey

shallow ford and the oldest stone bridge in the county show that the area had early beginnings. In the mill pond can be seen two of Turveys' best known inhabitants, Jonah and his wife, two stone statues brought to Turvey in 1844 from Ashridge House in Herfordshire. There has been a mill on the site of the present one since Domesday times. There was also a water-driven timber mill below. A flood gauge can be seen on the wall of the Three Fyshes recording a record flood.

The fine church of All Saints has Saxon origins, restored in the 19th century by Sir Gilbert Scott. During the restorations, a wall painting of the crucifixion dating back to the 13th century was uncovered in the Lady Chapel. The church has monuments to members of the Mordaunt family, fine brasses and a peal of eight bells. In the church can be seen a list of all the rectors of Turvey since 1085. There is also a parish map showing the ancient enclosures with names and the network of footpaths.

The Mordaunt family received the manor of Turvey from William the Conqueror. By 1662 they possessed nearly all the land in the village. Turvey Old Hall, now the site of Hall Farm, was the manor house. The Mordaunts supported the Roman Catholic faith and the heavy fines imposed on them eventually led to the break up of the estate. In 1786 the lands were sold; the manor of Turvey and the abbey lands were purchased by Mr Charles Higgins – later a part was sold to John

Higgins, a cousin, who built Turvey House in 1794. The attractive village of Turvey owes much to Higgins family, who rebuilt the tumbledown thatched cottages in the style we see today.

Charles Higgins took up residence in Abbey Farm, now known as Turvey Abbey. This had not housed a religious order but took its name from the land once owned by St James' Abbey in Northampton. The Abbey curiously is now home to an order of Benedictine nuns, so the religious connection has come full-circle. Visitors now come from far and wide on retreats and religious gatherings. The nuns work on beautiful religious embroidery and vestments.

One of the oldest buildings in Turvey is part of the group of three cottages in the centre. This was a coaching inn called The Tinker of Turvey, many centuries old. The Tinker of Turvey, Old Nell (his wife) and the dog are shown on the sign still surviving in Luton Museum. The building was altered in 1840 and recent changes have uncovered iron rings in the walls inside. Prisoners being taken to Bedford gaol were shackled to these while coach changes were made.

Turvey has a system of tunnels; one runs from the Abbey in a north-easterly direction. Another was discovered when the Victorian school was being converted. This ran along the back of the school towards Newton Lane. There is also reputed to be a tunnel from Turvey Old Hall to the church. Why they were built and where they all lead to is uncertain.

Lace was an important industry with lace schools and a centre for trading lace from the surrounding villages. At one time the village supported two blacksmiths, carpenters, builders, stonemasons, bakers, saddlers, etc.

Wander round the village and you will see many old cottages and attractive buildings. Find the shoe-scraper in the wall of Homelands on the High Street depicting Turvey Bridge supported by two herons. And don't miss the text from the Victorian school, now built into the cottage wall opposite Nell's Well in Newton Lane, and the matchstick figures on the rectory.

⌘ WHARLEY END

These days when one talks about Wharley End, one thinks mainly of Cranfield University which is a unique post-graduate teaching and research institution, founded as an RAF training establishment, transformed into the College of Aeronautics and now an academic centre of world-wide repute in many technology orientated fields.

The original Wharley End developed as an offshoot of the bigger village of Cranfield and from the Saxon founding of the parish until 1937 remained an End. Then came rumours of war and what had once been various small farms on the slightly dipping hilltop was transformed into a grass runway, with a groups of elegant Lutyens designed buildings clustered on the Wharley End side of the airfield. From the first, tree preservation and planting was encouraged, partly to provide camouflage in those early days, but later to make the site a haven of mature and maturing trees.

The core of the buildings at Wharley End is the Lutyens scheme for so many 1930s airfields, using excellent material, and unfussy design, which have worn well, and indeed, matured with dignity. Round the original group there has been a steady development of housing of every domestic style of British architecture since 1945, much of it undistinguished, but pleasant and well-maintained. What has been more interesting is the 'working' side of academic life. The buildings for that aspect have had to be technologically innovative, so there is every development from pre-war hangars to a Japanese inspired ecotechnology centre.

All this building came about because it was felt largely by Lord Kings Norton that the British aero-industry needed a permanent base from which to develop its technology. Lord Kings Norton and Sir Roy Fedden advised Sir Stafford Cripps that this was to be essential in the post-war world, and the RAF base at Wharley End was chosen in 1945 because it had an airfield with three runways, substantial buildings, and it is near Oxford, Cambridge and London.

From this very narrowly specialised beginning the College of Aeronautics expanded, gradually at first and then into many technological fields. The most rapid expansion occurred when the college (through the granting of a royal charter) attained university status in 1969 and became the Cranfield Institute of Technology, renamed Cranfield University in 1993.

The University has also benefited the surrounding community, bringing employment and increased prosperity to the area. Local people can take advantage of the many amenities on the campus, and farmers still cultivate cereals on the outer rim of the airfield.

The people who now live at Wharley End are largely students and their families. Many of them are from abroad and the strange life on a country campus surrounded by a windy stretch of Bedfordshire countryside must take some getting used to. However, this small 'united nations' in the middle of Bedfordshire has a harmony not usually seen in its larger counterpart.

⌘ WHIPSNADE

The parish of Whipsnade consists of three separate communities. The old village, with most of the houses surrounding the green, has changed little over many years, thanks to strict building restrictions. Then there is a large mobile-home park, and over a mile away and quite isolated the large modern houses in Old Hill Wood. On the west side of the green is the well-known Whipsnade Zoo, where on the hillside is the famous white chalk lion, which is lit up at night and can be seen for miles around.

The parish church, dedicated to St Mary Magdalene, is simple but beautiful. It is brick built, and the oldest part is the tower (c.1590), made from handmade bricks, some of the first manufactured in England since Roman times, the clay being dug and fired locally. The nave was built in 1719 in local bricks. The semicircular apse was added in 1860, so as a result the three parts of the church form a miniature history of Bedfordshire brickmaking.

A priest may have lived in the tower at one time, it is thought, and there is a window, now blocked up, which would have enabled vision to the entrance and the whole of the nave and altar. The chief feature of the furnishing is the superb 17th century pulpit and tester.

The Tree Cathedral, a church composed entirely of trees, with wide grass swards forming a nave and transepts, is a unique feature. It was the brainchild of the late E. K. Blyth, who began planting in 1930, working on until war came in 1939. The Tree Cathedral now belongs to the National Trust, and is cared for under the direction of the Trustees. An annual service is held during the summer, and other services are held by arrangement. It is a delightful, peaceful place in which to walk and enjoy nature.

Within the parish, on the Dunstable Downs, beside the road to Dunstable is a stone marking the highest point in Bedfordshire.

In times past local farms employed many of the men, while others walked to

The Tree Cathedral at Whipsnade

Dunstable for various jobs. Women did straw plaiting for the hat trade. They also collected herbs, hips, elderberries, blackberries, etc, which were sold to the pharmacists for a few pence, and went to local orchards for fruit gathering. The young girls went into domestic service. Later on, the Zoo employed both men and women, though not in large numbers.

⌘ WILLINGTON

The village of Willington is situated to the east of Bedford, with the river Great Ouse running alongside. It is said that the conquering Danes came up the river in their longships and cut out a harbour; certainly there is much evidence remaining today to support this theory. In the past the village was known mainly for agriculture and horticulture and had many nurseries. During the summer months the fields were ablaze with flowers of many different varieties and colours.

Standing impressively beside the parish church are two unusual 16th century buildings now owned by the National Trust, the magnificent dovecote and the

Willington's Tudor dovecote

Tudor stables, both built by Sir John Goswick with stone from the disused monastery at Newnham Priory.

The dovecote is rather grand with stepped gables and nesting boxes inside for 1,500 pigeons – a useful source of fresh meat in days gone by. It is now a home for nesting owls and kestrels! The stables (also built with stepped gables) have a large loft where the grooms could live. A horse in those days was essential for communication and hunting and some of the heavier horses were used on the farms. An inscription over John Goswick's tomb also says that he 'caused the work of rebuilding the church to be done'.

It is possible that all of this work was completed by 1541, the year in which Henry VIII visited John Gostwick, whom he had previously knighted. John Gostwick died in 1545. In the church is a replica of the helmet worn by him on the 'Field of the Cloth of Gold'. He was Master of the Horse to Henry VIII.

⌘ WOBURN

Although it is now a village, Woburn still has the status of a town, and is steeped in history.

The town hall still stands in the middle of the village. Whereas it was originally a stately market house, three storeys high, built about 1737, it was pulled down in 1830 and a new two-storey building was erected. In 1974 the Marquess of Tavistock restored the building yet again, converting the ground floor into offices and making an upper floor as a hall for recreation purposes.

As far as industry is concerned Woburn has had its fair share in the past. One such is the printing and bookbinding firm established prior to 1827 by Stephen Dodd, later known as the Drakeloe Press.

The school in Woburn has a very long history. Built in 1582 by Francis, Earl of Bedford, it had two storeys. Thirty-five boys were to be instructed in reading, writing and accounts. In 1822 the school accommodated 150 boys. In 1825 a school for girls commenced and they were taught needlework and lace-making.

Of course, Woburn is well known because of its association with the Dukes of Bedford and Woburn Abbey. The welfare of the town greatly benefited from the medical care brought to them by Mary, Duchess of Bedford, better known as the 'Flying Duchess'. In 1903 she built a hospital on the outskirts of the town in Leighton Street, known as the Woburn Clinic. The Duchess worked there as a theatre sister and radiologist and during the First World War it was used for the treatment of wounded soldiers. Soon after the tragic death in 1937 of the Duchess, the hospital was closed and the building used as a hostel by the College of Aeronautics, Cranfield. However, in 1967 the Woburn Clinic was taken over by the Bedfordshire Education Committee. It is now called Maryland College and is a residential college for adult education.

In the east wall of the south aisle of the new church is a stained glass window,

Woburn's Georgian High Street

installed in 1938 to the memory of the Flying Duchess. The window depicts St Francis of Assisi and no fewer than 58 birds – said to be one of every species to be found in Woburn Park at that time.

Tradition says that Sir Francis Staunton rebuilt the tower of the old church early in the 17th century, using stone from the church at Birchmore, and that the buildings which stand on the site of the old chapel-of-ease in Woburn High Street are the tower of 1830 and the mortuary chapel which was built in 1865. This was in use until 1980. It was then made redundant. Extensive repairs were done, both inside and outside, and the building is now used as a Heritage Centre.

When the church was pulled down, a new church was built in Park Street by William, 8th Duke, between 1865 and 1868. Underneath the church is a large crypt, originally meant as a burial place for the Russell family, but never used for that purpose, serving instead as a meeting place and function room.

Twelve almshouses were built in 1760 from a bequest given by Sir Francis Staunton to the 4th Duke. In 1968 they were converted into flatlets for retired parishioners. They were renamed Staunton House.

⌘ YIELDEN

Yielden is set in the extreme north of Bedfordshire and in fact part of the parish boundary is the Northamptonshire-Bedfordshire county border. It is a small parish of approximately 2,000 acres, almost entirely agricultural land.

Yielden's main claim to fame is its motte and bailey castle, a large mound which dominates the village. It was once the site of a Norman castle built in the 12th century but the historical interest in the site goes back to the 1st century, when it was believed to be the scene of a battle between the Iceni and the Romans. The castle has now disappeared, although an excavation made in the 1950s revealed the presence of masonry from the castle, but the original mound surrounded by its moat is still clearly visible.

The name of Yielden causes confusion in the village as there are three spellings in current usage, Yielden, Yelden and Yeldon, which makes life confusing for visitors trying to find it on the map. One of the earliest recorded spellings of the name was Giveldene, but it has been agreed by the Parish Council that the name should be spelt Yielden.

The parish church of St Mary is a Norman church dating back to the 12th century, although many parts of it have been rebuilt over the centuries. It is said that in the mid-17th century the rector at that time, William Dell, allowed John Bunyan to preach from the pulpit on Christmas Day. As John Bunyan was not ordained, William Dell was dismissed as the rector for allowing 'a tinker from Bedford' to preach.

In the 19th century lace making was one of the most flourishing trades in the village. According to a census taken in 1861 there were 18 girls under the age of 12 and 59 women all making pillow lace for sale and for export to America.

Meandering through the village is the river Til, which causes excitement during heavy rain, as it is prone to flooding. According to the record books there was a flood in 1912 when the village was under 5 feet of water in places. The drainage system has been updated so that, although it still floods at times, it is less severe.

Nowadays village life is very quiet with most people having to travel out of the village for work. With no school or shop the village lacks a central meeting place, but nevertheless Yielden still manages to thrive.